EMPOWERMENT OF
WOMEN AND GIRL CHILD

Empowerment of Women and Girl Child

Anupama Bishnoi
Manju Dahiya
Indu Grover

ANMOL PUBLICATIONS PVT. LTD.
NEW DELHI - 110 002 (INDIA)

ANMOL PUBLICATIONS PVT. LTD.
4374/4B, Ansari Road, Daryaganj
New Delhi - 110 002
Ph.: 23261597, 23278000
Visit us at: www.anmolpublications.com

Empowerment of Women and Girl Child

First Published, 2005

ISBN 81-261-2215-3

PRINTED IN INDIA

Published by J.L. Kumar for Anmol Publications Pvt. Ltd., New Delhi - 110 002 and Printed at Mehra Offset Press, Delhi.

Contents

Preface

The status of Women and Children all over the world has become a focus of national and international concern. Women's empowerment includes both a personal strengthening and enhancement of life chances, and collective participation in efforts to achieve equality of opportunity and equity between different genders, ethnic groups, social classes and age groups. From the Fifth Plan onwards many new programmes were included in the National Plans for the upliftment of the poor, particularly for Women and Children.

Since Independence, the Government of India's policies for Womens' Development have evolved in emphasis, from an initial welfare oriented approach to the current focus on development and empowerment. Empowerment of Women is a primary objective of the Tenth Plan. Women can be the primary agents for empowering individuals to transform society. They alone can inculcate in their children the self-esteem and respect for others essential for the advancement of civilization.

The present endeavour focuses on impact and empowerment of developmental programmes for mother and girl child in Haryana State. The study is a humble attempt and provides valuable insight in developmental programmes for mother and girl child in terms of existing knowledge and impact of selected developmental programmes, constraints affecting the knowledge, attitude and utilization of programme benefits.

It is hoped that this book will be useful and informative for scholars, researchers, Government and Non-Government agencies for planning and implementing programmes and policies. It would also help the planners to strengthen these programmes and facilities and give guidelines to other organizations involved in empowerment of Women and Children.

Anupama Bishnoi
Manju Dahiya
Indu Grover

August, 2004

Abbreviations

ABAD	Apni Beti Apna Dhan
AWW	Anganwadi Worker
BC	Backward Class
BPL	Below Poverty Line
BSY	Balika Samridhi Yojana
CDPO	Child Development Project Officer
DRDA	District Rural Development Agency
ICDS	Integrated Child Development Services
IVP	Indira Vikas Patra
MO	Medical Officer
NMBS	National Maternity Benefit Scheme
SC	Scheduled Caste
SMO	Senior Medical Officer

1

Introduction

Today's girl child is tomorrow's woman. If tomorrow's woman is to become an equal partner with man, there is a great need to accord the girl child her rightful share of dignity and opportunity today. Her physical, mental, emotional, intellectual and spiritual development will determine the quality of life of her family and generation to come. Although, the girl child has a natural biological advantage over the boy, yet in India, social disadvantage outweighs the genetic advantage of girls. As per 2001 Census, there are 495.7 million women. Approximately more than a quarter of India's population comprises of girls upto the age of 19 years. In the country, every year, 12 million girls are born, 3 million do not survive to see their 15th birthday. About one-third of these deaths are in the first year of life. It is estimated that every sixth female death is due to gender discrimination.

There is a strong gender bias in Indian society which idolizes son. As a result of customs, rituals and traditional practices girls are denied optimal opportunities for growth and development and treated as "lower child" (Amin, 2001). Girl child in India is subjected to 'inequality', 'disparity' and 'neglect'. Gender based inequalities permeate the very fabric of the social and cultural environment and the value system. Equality of opportunities between the sexes is enshrined in the Indian Constitution but it is still a distant dream and not a reality as far as women are concerned.

Since Independence, the Government of India (GOI) policies for women's development have evolved in emphasis, from an initial welfare oriented approach to the current focus on development and empowerment. Significant changes occurred in the mid-1980s with the Seventh Five Year Plan, which operationalize the concern for women's equality and empowerment and focussed on inculcating confidence among women, generating awareness of their rights and privileges, training them for economic activity and employment and bringing them into the mainstream of national development.

The Eighth Five Year Plan (1992-97) made a shift from development to empowerment of women. A number of measures have been taken by government in this direction for social and economic emancipation of women. The Ninth Plan Document (1997-2002) also lays emphasis on the participation of people in the planning process and the promotion of self-help groups. Empowerment of women is the ninth primary objective of the Ninth Plan. The Tenth Plan reinforces this commitment.

The process of women's empowerment is multidimensional. It enables women to realize their full potential and empower them in all spheres of life. Empowerment as a concept, therefore, encompasses their political empowerment, economic independence and social upliftment (Kant, 2001). The concept of empowerment of mother and girl child as a goal of development projects and programme has been gaining wider acceptance. A salient feature of the term empowerment is that it contains within it the word 'POWER'. This power operates in various fields of life as economic, social, political, religious, educational etc. Successive and continual denial of two of the most important sources of power i.e. education and economic independence has resulted in large scale powerlessness among women. Global Conference on Women's Empowerment highlighted the empowerment as the surest way of making them as partners in development (Chatterji, 1988). Empowerment, therefore, is a process which enables women to realize their identity and power in all aspects of life. It enables to have more access to knowledge and resources, greater autonomy in decision-making, greater ability to plan their time, free them from clutches of irrelevant customs, traditions and practices. "Empowerment and education are the keys to building self-esteem necessary for girls to understand and assert their rights and to act on behalf of their own advancement". Empowerment is power that stems from knowledge and skill acquired, action taken and their inner strength gained from educational experience (Nagarajan, 1998).

Mother and girl child are the greatest asset of any nation. They constitute about 70 per cent of the population of the country. Mothers can be the primary agents for empowering individuals to transform society. They alone can inculcate in their children the self-esteem and respect for others essential for the advancement of civilization. The low status of mother and girl child is seen to stem from low economic status, consequent dependence and lack of decision making power. They lag behind due to several socio-economic, cultural and political impediments. The declining male female sex ratio which stood at 1000 : 865 in 1991 and 1000: 861 in 2001 at State level i.e. Haryana that is second lowest in country is incidence of negative sex ratio, higher female child mortality rate, lesser access to food, health, education and family resources, early marriage and denial of legal rights to inheritance etc. The extremely important indicator of girl child status is the adverse sex ratio, with males outnumbering females by almost 10 per cent in all the States and this adverse sex ratio has been gradually getting worse over the years. The neglect and discrimination of the girl child are extensively and deeply rooted in a complex set of social, cultural and historical factors (Anonymous, 1990).

The culmination of growing concern for the girl child being subjected to inequality, disparity and neglect manifested in the decision to observe 1990 as the SAARC Year of the Girl Child. In spite of various constitutional safeguards and the National Plan of Action for the SAARC Decade of the Girl Child (1991-2000 A.D.) the basic gender disparities persist. National Plan of Action for children's goals and objectives are centered around a range of activities for the development of girl child and adolescent girls (NPA, 1992). There are a number of girl specific and mother and girl child related programmes implemented by both Central and State Governments.

In the Ninth and Tenth Five Year Plans, children are at the top of national agenda with a focus on gender equity. The major strategy in the Plan is to arrest the declining sex ratio, and eliminate problem of female foeticide and infanticide through two prolonged strategies of both direct and indirect measures. The focus is on improving quality of health services and early detection of health and nutrition problems among children, especially the girl child. Also, importance is being accorded to health and nutritional adequacy, nutritional status of mother and girl child, dietary intake and prevention of deficiency diseases. Gender bias results in lower health standard among girls. Male babies were breast-fed longer than the female babies. Mothers and girls in rural areas had low priority in getting share of family food (Chowdhary, 1990).

Even after over 50 years of Independence and constant efforts on the part of Government and various other national and international organizations, the girl child is still unwanted, suffers denial and discrimination throughout her childhood to perceive herself as second class and to accept and except negative status. While it cannot be denied that progress indeed has been made, but due to lack of motivation and felicitations, it has remained negligible or biased towards men.

Therefore, the present study was planned with a view to assess the impact of development programmes for empowerment of mother and girl child with the following objectives:

(i) To assess the impact of developmental programmes on empowerment of mother and girl child.

(ii) To identify constraints faced by beneficiaries in utilization of developmental programmes for mother and girl child.

Limitations of the Study

The study has obvious limitations of sample size, time, money and other resources. The study does not claim to generalize the findings for other developmental programmes as this is confined to only 3 selected developmental programmes for empowerment of mother and girl child in Fatehabad district, Harayana State.

However, the study is a humble attempt and provides valuable insight into the developmental programmes, existing knowledge of mother and girl child, impact of selected developmental programmes, constraints affecting the knowledge, attitude and utilization of programme benefits.

Scope of the Study

Integrated Child Development Services (ICDS) is the first countrywide programme. Specific developmental programmes for mother and girl child run under ICDS for below poverty line families, has generated considerable interest among planners and representatives implementing agencies. The findings of the present study may provide a guideline to the Government and Non-government agencies for new programmes and policies.

The identified problems and given suggestions would help the policy makers for intervention programmes in the villages. The research can help the planners to strengthen these programmes and facilities and can also give guidelines to other organizations involved in empowerment of mother and girl child.

2

Review of Literature

This chapter endeavours to present a critical review of the important research findings relevant to the topic of the study. Keeping in view the objectives of the study, the review has been presented under the following sub-heads.

Status of Girl Child

Rohtagi (1983) concluded that the girl child should not be deprived of the rudiments of basic education and should be allowed to enjoy her childhood, be trained for self-reliance not to break up our cherished joint family system but to strengthen it by responsible parenthood of bringing health, harmony and happiness in her new home.

Mathur (1984) revealed that the parents always pray for a son and the situation is worse in rural areas. Preference for boys or girls is deep-rooted in the psyche of the people and ingrained in the social, cultural and economic thinking through the centuries.

Anonymous (1987) revealed that the girl child bears the brunt of negative attitude as reflected in their declining sex-ratio, lower life expectancy, higher female infant mortality, lower nutritional status which is worst in north and north-west India.

Habibullah (1987) concluded that parents get the girls married to early for fear of society, dowry or family circumstances, and in the aim to marry off as earliest as possible, they do not pay enough attention to the health, nutrition and education of their daughters.

Sharma (1987) reported that marriage, and not education was considered important for girls, most of whom were married too early in life. But the scenario is fast changing with the age of consent going upto that prescribed by law due to the spread of education and other development programmes.

Salvi (1989) concluded that nutritional level of female infant is much worse than their male counterparts, moreover, female children receive hardly any medical attention when they are ill, the picture of girl child in education being equally disturbing.

Anonymous (1990) reported that the extremely important indicator of girl child status is the adverse sex ratio, with males outnumbering females by almost 10 per cent in all the States and this adverse sex ratio has been gradually getting worse over the years. The neglect and discrimination of the girl child are extensively and deeply rooted in a complex set of social, cultural and historical factors.

Chaudhary (1990) found that gender bias results in lower health standard among girls. Male babies were breast-fed longer than the female babies. Women and girls in rural areas had low priority in getting share of family food.

Jain (1990) reported that to a large extent the prejudice against girls arises from the fear over their security right from time they are born and all through their childhood, girlhood, adolescence and womanhood. Poverty, together with social attitudes, has denied her the rights due to her as a child and as a human being.

Kulshreshtha (1990) revealed that changing patterns not with standing, even today's life for the girl child is a never ending hurdle race. They become victims of orthodox beliefs and treated as an inferior human being governed by social norms prescribed by male dominated society—to be treated as a burden of parents, to be deprived of opportunities in life. She faces oppressions and suppressions and taught to sacrifice her self either as mother or a wife.

Kumar (1990) reported that without proper education, the

joys of a beautiful childhood are denied to the girl child. In our world, more than 100 million children of school age, 60 per cent of them girls, never step inside a classroom.

Kumar (1990) reported that there are millions of girl children in world who do not enjoy basic human rights. They have no childhood and no future from a very tender age, they have to act like adults, work very hard and contribute towards their family income yet most of the times they do not even get a day's square meal, and are the most vulnerable victims of malnutrition and disease.

Bhogle (1991) reported that there is a major significant sex-discrimination in the areas of age of sending to school, choice of school and future aspirations of the girl child.

Ghosh (1991) marshals a whole range of statistical data to substantiate the girl child's life time of deprivation and discrimination in India. The declining sex ratio, the pathetic nutritional status, the discriminatory for supply, higher morbidity and mortality are indicators of this.

Ghosh (1991) revealed that the school enrolment for age 11-14 years is 29 per cent for girls as against 54 per cent for boys and the figure drops to 14 per cent of girls of 15-17 years as against 28.6 per cent for boys. The dropout rate is very high among the girls.

UN Convention (1992) India ratified UN Convention on the rights of the child. Article 2 of the convention stresses on gender equality by starting that rights set forth in convention are for all children irrespective their sex.

Amin (2001) revealed that there is a strong gender bias in Indian society which idolizes son. As a result of customs, rituals and traditional practices girls are denied optimal opportunities for growth and development and treated as lesser child. This attitude is reflected in the low literacy level of women and higher dropout rates in girls.

Azim (2001) reported gender disparities unfavourable to

women in terms of all sorts of deprivations including education, health care, maternal medical attendance, economic assets, political participation and decision-making, share in earned income, autonomy in fertility related decisions are more pronounced in India.

Chandermohan (2001) envisaged that girl child experiences discrimination in all aspects of life and the existing socio-cultural practices make it difficult for her to overcome the handicaps posed by her unequal status. Socio-cultural biases combined with poverty, weigh heavily on adolescent girls who marry early and bear children at a young age and who work for long hours in the home and outside, with unequal access to health and nutrition, education and other opportunities.

Empowerment and Development

Gangrade (1966) observed after analysing the results of a critical study of women's participation in a centre of Delhi's villages, that for some developmental activities specially those related to home and family, the real workers are women. Without their cooperation job cannot be done.

Patel (1982) revealed that the success of any rural development programme depends on the acceptance of the programme by the people. For this purpose, it is necessary that the people are involved in the programme right from the stage of planning.

Trivedi (1982) envisaged that due to lack of regular guidance and supervision of the rural programmes, a good programme is not implemented well enough and the poor loose interest and confidence. Therefore, proper arrangements of adequate capital in tune for right purpose to the right families is the basic to the success of the programme, and those would gather enough mass for people's participation in them.

Chatterji (1988) reported that global conference on women's empowerment highlighted the empowerment as the surest way of making them as partners in development.

Anonymous (1991) reported that the United Nation International Children's Emergency Fund (UNICEF) priority areas will be development of the girl child, better care for her and improving the position of women which in turn would improve the conditions for children.

NPA (1992) National Plan of Action for children goals and objectives are centered around a range of activities for the development of girl child and adolescent girls.

Chaudhary (1993) pointed out that Eighth Five Year Plan (1992-97) made a shift from development to empowerment of women. A number of measures have been taken by government in this direction for social and economic emancipation of women.

Sood (1994) reported that policies, programmes and areas of development for women and girl child are lacking. It is apathy in continuing the traditional discriminatory ways in the process which impairs the positive effects of the programmes.

Chandra (1996) stated that women need to be empowered at earliest. Empowerment has to be in terms of information, knowledge, skills besides social, economic and political empowerment.

Joshi (1996) revealed that women empowerment would improve the health status. Enhancement of women's education and promotion of women mobility will enable them to take decision about reproductive health and avail of health services by themselves. Besides, women should be empowered to take decision about the number of children, use of family planning methods and their own reproductive, health care. Moreover, economic empowerment of women is also very important for raising their status in the society.

Nagarajan (1998) stated the empowerment is power that stems from new knowledge and skill acquired, action taken and their inner strength gained from educational experiences.

NIPCCD (2000) reports found that most of the issues concerning adult women are linked to the problems of the girl child right from infancy to adolescence, the development of girl child has become the focus of attention of all development endeavours.

Agarwal (2001) revealed that there is a need for comprehensive and holistic policy for women. This would enable the country to fulfil the constitutional mandate of women's equality and objective of women's total involvement in national development.

Kant (2001) observed that the process of women's empowerment is multidimensional. It enables women to realize their full potential and empower them in all spheres of life. Empowerment as a concept, therefore, encompasses their political empowerment, economic independence and social upliftment.

Sharma (2001) reported that slight increase in the number of women is the first flicker of hope that women's empowerment programmes are having some material impact on condition of women.

Singh (2001) observed that women means the opportunity and ability to assert their rights and fight for justice. Development also means real improvement in the socio-economic conditions of women. Those in authority should have the will to enforce all development programmes which if done in right earnest can go a long way in empowering women.

Sundaram (2001) concluded that women in India, because of their subordinate status in society, miss many opportunities especially due to their limited access to crucial inputs like credit. Women have become victims of deprivation, discrimination and atrocities.

Knowledge about Development Programmes

Paranjpe and Bhagwat (1986) found that general level of knowledge about ICDS programme was very poor. The source of getting knowledge were informal, such as observation by self or casual discussions with the anganwadi workers or the neighbours.

However, nutrition was the most widely known (77%) but not the most appreciated service.

Dubey and Pandey (1987) revealed a change in knowledge of various aspects of health and child care due to radio broadcasts, even in the non-listener group of women. Radio listening followed by group discussion was found to be more effective in imparting knowledge to women.

Sangwan *et al.* (1987) concluded that various community facilities be made available in villages and women should be made aware of these facilities to help them from developmental programmes. The awareness may ultimately lead to utilization of these facilities for participating in income generating activities.

Kumar *et al.* (1988) revealed that three fourth (74.5%) respondents were aware of availability of existing services and 69.1% of them could state one or more items of mother and child health care existing among rural areas.

Narayanan (1989) found that level of knowledge was higher in the experimental groups than in the control groups. Most of the beneficiaries were not aware or clear about Government's role. Most of the beneficiaries had usually contacts with anganwadi workers, helper and mid-wife. They had no contacts with Child Development Project Officers (CDPOs) and supervisors.

Padmanabhan *et al.* (1989) found that mother's knowledge about health was poor. It was better in areas covered by ICDS as compared to non-ICDS area. Father's involvement was very much limited. Whereas the health education component was not as effectively delivered by medical and paramedical personnel as envisaged by them.

Sitalakshmi and Jotimani (1994) concluded that participation in development programme appeared to have raised the image of women in family and they were being consulted or given sole responsibility of taking the decision on various familiar aspects.

Attitude toward Developmental Programmes

Sud (1982) elucidated that due to less enthusiastic attitude of the field level workers as well as the people about their success, some of the well conceived projects have failed to yield desired results.

Bhatnagar and Singhal (1984) conducted a study in Udaipur and found that majority of the participants (90%) had favourable attitude, out of which about nineteen per cent had the most favourable attitude. Only 10 per cent participants were found to have unfavourable attitude towards ICDS programme.

Rajula Devi (1986) found that the attitude of the beneficiaries towards the anti-poverty programme varies a great deal. Eighty per cent of the poor were satisfied with the programme. The percentage of dissatisfaction is more among other castes other than scheduled castes because of more benefits provided to them.

Natarajan (1989) conducted study in Government Rayapeetah Hospital, Madras to find out the attitude of mothers towards antenatal services and family planning. Overwhelmingly, majority of women (98.35%) were aware of significance of antenatal care. Seventy five per cent of women were having accepted family planning methods.

Kumar and Ramaiah (1992) revealed that majority of beneficiaries have more favourable attitude, which was followed by medium (46%) and less favourable attitude. As majority of beneficiaries were directly involved in development progarmme, it was likely to have favourable attitude.

Utilization of Development Programmes

Gupta *et al.* (1979) interviewed the community members and revealed that a good number of beneficiaries were aware of services utilized by them and were satisfied. However, a lot of scope exists for increasing the participation of the community in the Anganwadi so as to ease the pressure of work on Anganwadi workers.

Jayawena (1979) reported that women themselves lack adequate motivation to utilize even the limited facilities available to them. Their living conditions exclude them from participating in useful programmes and thereby help to perpetrate their social and economic deprivation.

Kaur and Narwal (1988) found that majority (66%) of the respondents had low level of utilization, 23 per cent had medium and 11 per cent had high level of utilization of the immunization practices.

Dhar (1989) stated that reasons for poor participation by women included lack of awareness of the services offered or of their significance, lack of space for a women's group to function at the Anganwadi centres and inconvenient timings which clash with women's hours of work.

Tandon and Bhattacharya (1989) revealed gross under utilization of ante-natal care services. The degree of utilization was significantly related to education of woman and her husband. Whereas 15 per cent of illiterate women used the services, 58 per cent of the literate women did so. Utilization was also related to caste of the couple, 58% of the upper caste were users and as much as 85% of the lower caste were non-users.

Tripathi *et al.* (1990) studied that more than 15% of the total beneficiaries of the IRDP misutilized the assistance. This was due to lack of proper supervision by the block staff.

Rao (1997) studied that income carried by majority women under programmes were spent on family, in consultation with husband, very few women mentioned that they had actual control on money earned.

Sharma *et al.* (1998) concluded that neighbours were considered important sources of information followed by friends and relative. Therefore, the neighbours and friends could be treated as important sources of information.

Impact of Developmental Programmes

Chikara (1982) revealed that mortality was more frequent in the age group 1 month to 1 year, with whom Anganwadi workers has hardly any contact.

Mehendate *et al.* (1985) concluded that ICDS had definite impact on the health and nutritional status of children as the decrease in the incidence of malnutrition.

Chamola *et al.* (1986) reported the impact of development programme on income of the respondents, that there is an increase in income in the first 3 years and then starts declining. Beneficiaries used a major part of the additional income for consumption purposes.

Singhal and Goyal (1986) indicated that decisions related to expenditure on food, clothing, children's education, savings, investments, family ceremonies and festivals were taken jointly by husband and wife in majority of the families followed by a joint decision of all family members.

Rao (1987) reported that the achievement in case of development programmes is quite dismal. The actual number of beneficiaries turned out to be far less than the targeted number. Lot of imagination and expertise are required to plan the development programmes.

Nair (1989) revealed that there was a great awareness of the programme among the tribal women irrespective of their educational level. Respondents' attitudes to some extent were influenced by their educational level. The health and nutrition practices were influenced by the educational, income and occupational level of the respondents.

Vidyalata (1989) tried to show the impact of development programme on the status of women and concluded that it had resulted in increased perception of using property, personal earning and keeping their earning with themselves. So, it has helped in improving the status of women.

Sundri and Kamalabai (1991) revealed that all the respondents of development programme reported that the scheme had augmented their income improved their standard of living, helped them to repay their debt and improved in their health condition.

Sood (1994) observed that impact of development programme has not yet been augmenting on women. It is but essential that proper execution of projects is carried out thoroughly to achieve the development goals.

Aneja and Chhikara (1995) analysed that health and nutrition education component of ICDS programme certainly had positive impact on knowledge of its beneficiaries regarding aspects of prenatal care, family planning etc.

Prasad (1995) observed that allocation made in development programme for rural development should be increased substantially to make perceptible impact on poverty alleviation programmes.

Venketswara and Venkatramana (1995) revealed that about 19 per cent of the respondents reported that their social status had increased while for remaining 81 per cent there was no change in their social status after being provided with the benefits. Most of the beneficiaries, accepted an increase in their income after implementation of various developmental programmes.

Planning Department, Government of Haryana (2000) a survey conducted by Economic and Statistical Organization on "Apni Beti Apna Dhan" revealed that 93.7% of the targets of assisting beneficiaries were achieved during the year 1997-98.

Constraints faced in Utilization of Developmental Programmes

Mehta (1971) reported the leaders view that bigger land owners, rich people, landlords, higher caste groups and friends of the block officials are the most benefited groups from the development programmes. The labourers, the poor, the non-agriculturists and the lower caste groups seem to be the least benefited from these programmes.

Shekhar (1975) reported a lack of coordination between health care delivery personnel and development officials. It was reported that the various coordination committees can be made more effective and successful if adequate measures are taken to strengthen the organizational base, especially at field level.

Sethi (1976) observed a lack of coordination between state, district, block level administration and between different departments, involved in procurement and distribution of food supplement.

Ramachandran (1977) reported that planning of development programme was done at state level leaving very little scope for local planning at district level. Job orientation was lacking for every category of staff and supervision at different levels was found to be superficial. Records were poorly designed and maintained. Existing manpower and other resources were not adequately utilized.

Bhatnagar and Shahin (1979) observed that field level workers were not able to create a link between peripheral workers and the community.

Freire (1979) reported that beneficiaries should also be involved in the monitoring process. They should not be treated a "mere objects of the study but as participants in the enquiry".

Anonymous (1980) reported that there is a need to increase coordination between various levels of administrative personnel and between personnel from different departments, so that the programme can be planned and implemented in a truly integrated fashion.

Jorapur (1981) reported that the food distributed through Integrated Child Development Scheme is not distributed regularly, on account of lack of proper organization of distributional machinery, administrative bottleneck, procedural rigidity and also personal weaknesses of either the Anganwadi workers or her helper. The casual problems in the distribution of food are lack of sufficient food.

Kamath (1981) pointed out that the social taboos and traditions have stood in the way of ready acceptance of diets ideal in calories and nutrients.

Chakraborti *et al.* (1984) revealed that a number of socio-psychological factors acting as barriers to adoption behaviour are joint family structure, lower subcaste, illiteracy, lack of formal participation in village bodies, non-accessibility of media, lack of urban contact or occupational mobility, dearth of political knowledge, fatalism and lack of secular orientation.

Verma (1987) observed that linkage between researchers, extension personnel and utilizing systems was quite weak. No satisfactory built in mechanism existed for effective linkage and communication amongst researchers and extension workers of ICDS and rural women.

Dev and Lal (1989) revealed that according to supervisors and CDPOs the major constraints were inadequate knowledge of ICDS programme, lack of proper training of Anganwadi worker, infrequent contacts with community due to lack of transport facilities, caste rivalries, party politics and inadequate effort by ICDS functionaries to motivate beneficiaries.

Balishter and Umesh Chandra (1990) reported that several problems which caused inadequate impact on income generation under development programme were delay in disbursal of loan, delay in releasing subsidy, bribe taken by implementing agencies.

Kaptan (1994) reported that lack of motivation from family members was a major constraint. Due to this, they find great difficulty in combating the opposition first from the family members and then from society at various levels.

Ponnuraj (1994) reported that in India the centrally funded maternal and child health programme has largely failed to recognize the needs vary between different groups of people, and has consequently not secured the desired level of community participation.

Quigley and Ebrahim (1995) reported that there are many factors with constraint of the involvement of women in health activities. In many developing societies women have a relatively low social and economic status and yet they are expected to fulfil their multiple role—despite their limited access to information, education and opportunities.

Chidambaran and Themonzhi (1998) studied that general/ personal constraints, excessive tensions and challenges as endorsed by majority of respondents was the common constraint. About 72 per cent of the respondents expressed excessive burden of work and responsibility as one of the major constraints followed by lack of leisure time.

3

Materials and Methods

This chapter deals with methodological steps adopted in carrying out the present study. The research procedures followed are presented under the following heads:

Locale of the Study

For the present study Fatehabad district of Haryana State was selected purposively due to the easy accessibility and convenience.

SAMPLING PROCEDURE

This sampling procedure is given in Fig. 3.1.

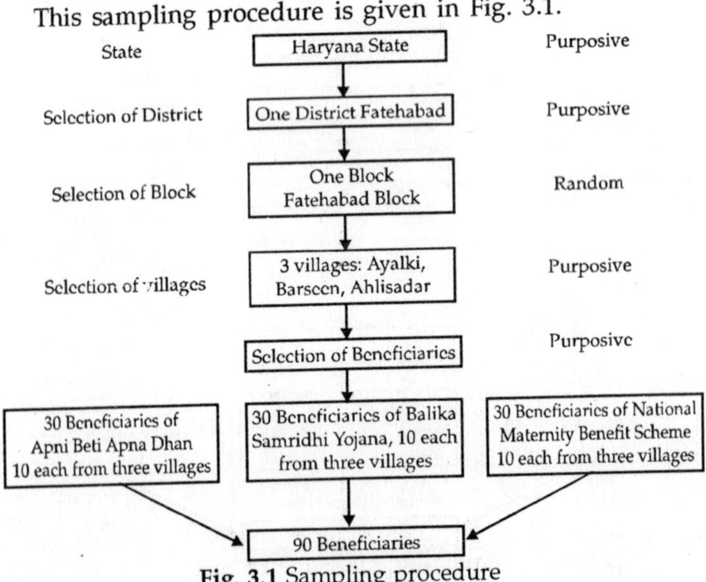

Fig. 3.1 Sampling procedure

Selection of Programmes

A list of developmental programmes operating for mother and girl child in Fatehabad district under Integrated Child Development Services (ICDS) was obtained from Child Development Project Officer (CDPO) office. All the three programmes namely, Apni Beti Apna Dhan (ABAD), Balika Samridhi Yojana (BSY) and National Maternity Benefit Scheme (NMBS) were selected which are in operation in Fatehabad district.

Selection of District

Out of the nineteen districts of Haryana, Fatehabad district was selected purposively as it is one of the newly carved out district from Hisar and Sirsa district in Haryana and also due to the convenience.

Selection of Block

From selected district, out of 5 blocks, one block i.e. Fatehabad block was selected randomly.

Selection of Villages

There are 63 villages in Fatehabad block. Since the study aimed at assessing the impact of developmental programmes on empowerment of mother and girl child, information about the villages where programmes had been in operation atleast since the past three years was sought from the office of CDPO Fatehabad. From Fatehabad block, 3 villages namely Ayalki, Barseen and Ahlisadar were selected purposively on the basis of maximum number of beneficiaries in these programmes.

Selection of Beneficiaries

A list of beneficiaries of the selected villages who were beneficiaries of three selected development programmes was obtained from CDPO office, Fatehabad and also cross checked from Anganwadi centres of selected villages. One list per programme was prepared. From each list a matching sample of

30 beneficiaries per programme with 10 beneficiaries in each programme per village was drawn randomly. This included a sample of 30 beneficiaries of 'Apni Beti Apna Dhan', 30 of 'Balika Samridhi Yojana' and 30 of 'National Maternity Benefit Scheme'. In this way total of 90 beneficiaries constituted the sample for the present investigation.

VARIABLES AND THEIR MEASUREMENTS

Under this section, the instruments/techniques to measure the independent and dependent variables have been incorporated. A detailed account of these variables alongwith their measurement procedures is contained in the following table:

Table 3.1 Variables and their Measurements

Sl. No.	*Variables*	*Instrument used*
	Independent Variables	
	Socio-personal and Economic Variables	
1.	Age	Chronological
2.	Education	Schedule Developed
3.	Caste	Schedule Developed
4.	Family Type	Schedule Developed
5.	Family Size	Schedule Developed
6.	Family Occupation	Schedule Developed
7.	Family Income	Schedule Developed
8.	Land Holding	Schedule Developed
9.	Nutritional Status	Body Mass Index (Garrow, 1981)
10.	Ordinal Position of Girl Child	Schedule Developed
11.	Social Participation	Schedule Developed
12.	Constraints faced in utilization of benefits of developmental programme	Schedule Developed
Communication Variables		
13.	Mass Media Exposure	Schedule Developed

contd...

Sl. No.	*Variables*	*Instrument used*
14.	Sources of Information	Schedule Developed
15.	Sources of Motivation	Schedule Developed
	Dependent Variables	
(a)	Knowledge about Programme	Knowledge Inventory
(b)	Attitude towards Programme	Schedule Developed
(c)	Utilization of Programme Benefits	Schedule Developed
(d)	Impact of Programme	Impact Assessment Index

INDEPENDENT VARIABLES

Socio-personal and economic variables, communication variables constituted the independent variables for the purpose of the study.

1. Age

The chronological age of respondents at the time of interview was taken for the purpose of the study. On the basis of minimum and maximum age of the respondents were placed according to their age in two equal categories of young and middle age. Details of categories and scores is as follows:

Category	**Score**
Young (20-30 years)	1
Middle (30-40 years)	2

2. Education

Education was operationalized as the number of years of formal education acquired by the respondent and information was quantified as follows:

Category	**Score**
Illiterate	0
Primary	1
Middle	2
High School	3

3. Caste

Caste refers to class or distinct social order existing in society. The operational measure of caste as per was taken as depicted below:

Category	Score
General	1
Backward Class	2
Scheduled Caste	3

4. Family Type

It means whether a family is nuclear or joint. Nuclear family is composed of parents and children, whereas joint family is referred to one which was constituted by more than one parents together with their children. It was operationally measured. For the purpose of qualification, relative scores assigned were as follows:

Category	Score
Nuclear	1
Joint	2

5. Family Size

Family size refers to the total number of members in a family. The scores to measure the variable were as follows:

Category	Score
Small (upto 4 members)	1
Small (5-8)	2
Large (9 and more)	3

6. Family Occupation

It has been operationalized as the specific work which the head of the family or major members do to earn a livelihood. The occupation has been measured with the help of socio-economic status. The following scoring pattern was used:

Category	Score
Labour	1
Caste Occupation	2
Business	3
Independent Profession	4
Cultivation	5
Service	6

7. Family Income

Family income refers to the annual income of the family from all sources during a year. As the beneficiaries of the development programme under investigation were from Below Poverty Line (BPL) families as per criteria laid down by State Government (information collected from DRDA office), family as a unit having annual income from all sources including agriculture not more than Rs. 24,000 per annum is considered below poverty line family. The family income was studied under three equal categories as detailed below:

Category	Score
Extremely poor (upto Rs. 10,000)	1
Very poor (Rs. 10,000 to 20,000)	2
Poor (Rs. 20,000 to 25,000)	3

8. Land Holding

Land holding refers to the size of cultivated land possessed by the respondent's family. Land holding criteria laid down by the State Government (information collected from DRDA office) for BPL family of irrigated land not more than 2.5 acres and dry land not more than 5 acres was taken. Details of categories are as follows:

Category	Score
Landless	1
Marginal	2
Irrigated land (upto 2.5 acres]	3
Dry land (upto 5 acres)	4

9. Nutritional Status

Nutritional status refers to the state of health of an individual as determined by the utilization of food. Body Mass Index was used to measure the nutritional status of the mother. This is estimated on the basis of height and weight and calculated by using Quotelet Index (Q.I.).

$$Q.I = \frac{\text{Weight (kg)}}{\text{Height}^2\text{(m)}}$$

It was further measured by adopting three categories following scoring based on Garrow (1981).

Category	Score
Low wt. Normal (18.5-20.0)	1
Normal (20.0-25.0)	2
Obese Grade I (25.0-30.0)	3

10. Ordinal position of Girl Child

Ordinal position of the child refers to the birth order of the children of mother in family excluding the abortions and deaths. It was operationalized in terms of the number of children of beneficiary and also specific number of girl children based on the actual information. The benefit of the schemes is only extended upto three children. Categories devised are as under:

(a) Number of Children

Category	Score
1 to 2 children	1
3 Children	2
More than 3 children	3

(b) Specific number of Girl Children

Category	Score
One	1
Two	2
Three	3

11. Social Participation

It refers to the degree of involvement of respondents in formal organization either as a member or as an office bearer. It was measured with the help of schedule developed. The scoring pattern was used as follows:

Category	Score
No membership	0
Member of an Organization	1
Office bearer	2
Public leader	3

COMMUNICATION VARIABLES

12. Mass Media Exposure

It has been operationalized as the degree to which a respondent was exposed to the mass media such as radio, television, magazines and newspapers for obtaining information. The categories devised are:

Category	Score
No exposure	0
Radio	1
Television	2
Print Media	3

13. Source of Information

It is operationalized in terms of communication contacts of beneficiaries with different sources of information. Localite and cosmopolite sources were given sources of 1 and 2, respectively. The total scores obtained by each respondent were categorized into three categories of high, medium and low. Scoring was done as under:

Category	Score
Low (upto 12)	1
Medium (13-23)	2
High (24-35)	3

14. Source of Motivation

This refers to the source of motivation that inspired the beneficiaries for availing the benefit of the programme. The scoring procedure was same as for source of information. Scores are given as under:

Category	Score
Low (upto 12)	1
Medium (13-23)	2
High (24-35)	3

DEPENDENT VARIABLES

Dependent variables for the present study were knowledge, attitude, utilization of programme benefits and impact of developmental programmes on empowerment of mother and girl child. The method of measurement for each has been explained hereafter.

a) Knowledge about Programme

Knowledge about programme has been operationalized as level of knowledge of the respondents about the specific developmental programme. This was measured with the help of statements related with objectives and other details of the programme. The response against each statement was taken in 'Yes' or 'No' responses and score assigned were 'One' and 'Zero', respectively.

Based on the responses obtained against each items these were summated in order to obtain the total scores. The minimum and maximum score obtained was further divided into three equal categories of low, medium and high with score ranges as follows:

Category	Score
Low (0-4)	1
Medium (4-7)	2
High (7-10)	3

b) Attitude towards Programme

Attitude towards programme can be defined as the degree of positive or negative affect associated with some psychological object (Thurstone, 1946). An individual who has associated positive effect with some psychological object is said to have a favourable attitude and an individual who has associated negative effect with some psychological object would be said to have an unfavourable attitude towards the object. About 16 statements comprising of the content area were derived from relevant literature and discussion. Each item in the scale was provided with five point summated rating of Likert (1932). These were strongly favourable, neutral, unfavourable and strongly unfavourable. The scoring technique for favourable statements was 5, 4, 3, 2 and 1, respectively and for unfavourable statements, it was reversed.

Based on the responses obtained against each item, these were summated in order to obtain the total scores. The aggregate scores were then divided into three categories of favourable, somewhat favourable and unfavourable.

c) Utilization of Programme Benefits

Utilization programme benefits had been operationalized as

making full use of different types of services provided by running the developmental programmes and also included information such as procedural aspects, utilization of services provided at village level and change after availing benefit. For the measurement of these variables schedule was developed and scores were assigned accordingly.

Impact of the Programme

For the purpose of the present study, the impact has been operationalized as percentage change in knowledge, attitude and utilization of programme benefits of developmental programmes. It was measured by first measuring each of the three variables separately and then assessing the total impact. The same was measured on specifically designed index with the help of formula given below:

$$\text{Impact Assessment Index} = \frac{\Sigma fi \times ai}{N \times X \times Y \times Z} \times 100$$

where,

fi = Frequency in 1th cell

ci = Cell scores of 1th cell (product of corresponding scale values as presented in parenthesis on three dimensions in table

N = Total number of respondents

X (Knowledge) = Highest scale value on X dimension

Y (Attitude) = Highest Scale Value on Y dimension

Z (Extent of utilization) = Highest Scale Value on Z dimension

Constraints faced in utilization of benefits of developmental programmes

Constraints were operationalized as the obstacles which hindered the utilization of development programmes under study of the beneficiaries. For measuring the same, a schedule was developed. A list of statements comprising all possible constraints was prepared and after pre-testing, it was further edited and finalized. The constraints were studied under four categories i.e. organizational constraints, economic constraints, educational and communicational constraints and socio-cultural constraints. The response against each statement was taken in 'Yes' or 'No' response and score assigned were 'One' and 'Zero', respectively. Based on the responses against each statement these were summated.

3.5 Construction of Interview Schedule

A well-structured interview schedule was prepared in accordance with methodological procedures and objectives of the study. The same was pretested on 10 beneficiaries from a non-sampled village. Necessary changes were incorporated before finalization.

Data Collection

Data were personally collected by the researcher through interview method with the help of interview schedule.

Analysis of Data

The data were coded, tabulated and analysed by using frequency and percentage and statistical techniques.

4

Theoretical Frame and Organizational Pattern of Selected Developmental Programmes

In order to have a cognizant view of the developmental programmes for mother and girl child, a comprehensive attempt has been made in this chapter to present salient details of these programmes. To assess the theoretical frame and organizational pattern of the three selected development programmes namely, Apni Beti Apna Dhan, Balika Samridhi Yojana and National Maternity Benefit Schemes for mother and girl child, with special reference to the organizational setup at different levels with various authorities and their roles, eligibility criteria, financial assistance, procedure for applying and obtaining benefit are based on information collected through personal interviews with administrators and published reports. Details for each of these programmes viz. Apni Beti Apna Dhan, Balika Samridhi Yojana and National Maternity Benefit Scheme is presented separately hereafter.

1. APNI BETI APNA DHAN

'Apni Beti Apna Dhan' programme was introduced in Haryana State on 2nd October, 1994 coinciding with the 125th birth anniversary of Father of Nation, Mahatma Gandhi. Under this programme, financial assistance of Rs. 500/- as post delivery financial assistance (PDFA) is given to the mother and Rs. 2500/- are invested with Indira Vikas Patra for the newly born girl child. The main objective is:

- To raise the status of girl child in family and society and to honour the mother of girl child.

While the specific objectives are:

- To reduce demographic imbalance between sexes.
- To delay the age of marriage of girls to atleast 18 years.
- To reduce birth rate and improve reproductive health.
- To initiate the change in attitude of society towards girl child.

Assistance Provided

a) Mother

Under this programme, within 15 days of giving birth of girl child, Rs. 500/- is given in cash to the mother for her nutrition and recoupment of health.

b) Girl Child

Indira Vikas Patra of Rs. 2500/- are purchased in favour of girl child within 3 months of her birth. These cannot be encashed and are to be kept for a period of 18 years while this amount will increase to Rs. 25000/- on its maturity.

Beneficiaries

The benefits of the programme accrue to:

a) Girl children born in families below poverty line and are in the list of identified families available with DRDAs.

b) The families should not have more than three children including new born and parents have domicile of Haryana State.

Procedure for Applying and Obtaining the Benefit

It is the duty of Anganwadi worker in rural area to identify the pregnant women through house to house survey and monitor it till the birth of child. The application forms are collected by mother/father/guardian of the girl child of identified family for availing the benefit of Rs. 500/- for the mother of girl child as post-natal assistance from Anganwadi Centres in rural areas and Civil Hospital/Community Health Centre/Primary Health Centre/ Medical Officer in Urban areas. The required application forms are got filled in from the beneficiary family by the AWW in rural areas and forwarded to the Supervisor, ICDS and by Health Supervisor (female) in urban areas and forwarded to Civil Surgeon/SMO/MO Incharge of the area for the release of funds within 15 days of giving birth to the girl child.

For availing the benefit of Rs. 2500/- extended to the girl child the required application form is initially collected by any member of the family from Anganwadi centre in rural area and Health Supervisor (female) in urban area. The duly filled in form along with a copy of the certificate of birth of girl child is submitted to anganwadi worker in rural area and to SMO/MO in urban area. The Supervisor forwards the form to CDPO for sanction. The Indira Vikas Patra of Rs. 2500/- are purchased in favour of girl child within 3 months of birth of girl child and the IVP are issued and given to mother/father of the girl child.

Organizational Setup

The organizational setup is depicted in Fig. 4.1. The scheme is operated at State level and is being implemented both in urban and rural areas under ICDS programme. It can be observed that at the State level the Director, Women and Child Development Department, Haryana is the overall incharge of Apni Beti Apna Dhan, who is assisted by one Joint Director at the Head Office. He/she is responsible for planning/staffing at various levels and allocating budget. At the District level, Programme Officer is the authority for Supervision and guidance of the activities.

At the Block level, Child Development Project Officer is incharge and is responsible for the group activities. At a cluster of village level, Supervisor is incharge of 20 Anganwadi centres. The Anganwadi is a focal point for delivery of package of services

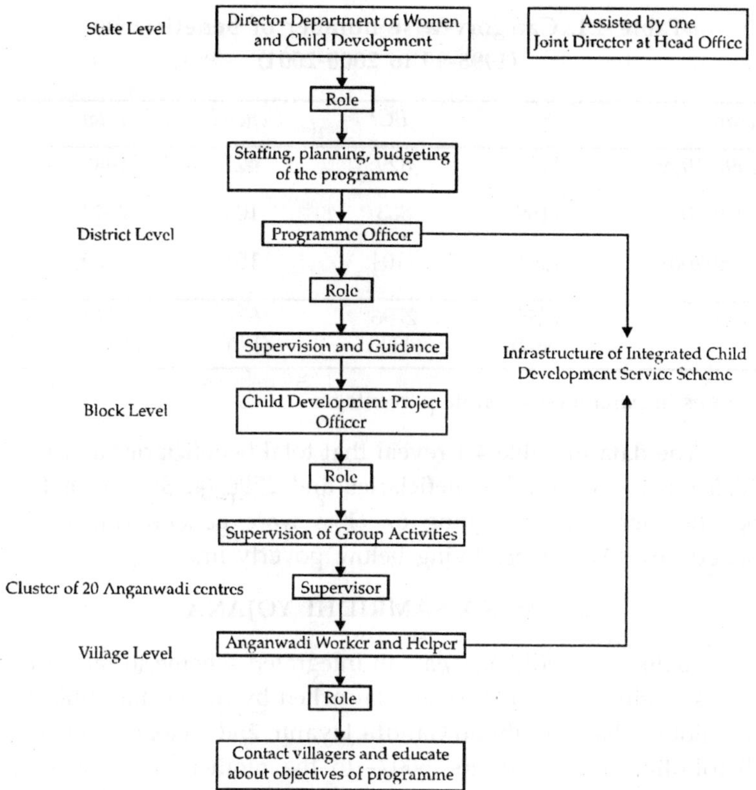

Fig. 4.1 Organisational setup of 'Apni Beti Apna Dhan' programme

to children and mothers right at their doorstep. An Anganwadi normally covers a population of about 1,000 in rural areas. The Anganwadi is run and managed by an Anganwadi worker. She is assisted by a Helper in organizing various services. Their job is to contact villagers frequently, maintenance of desired registers and educate mothers about objectives of the programme.

Number of Beneficiaries benefitted during the year 1998-99 to 2000-2001 in District Fatehabad

In all, 6548 beneficiaries were assisted during the year 1998-99 to 2000-2001. The category-wise number of beneficiaries assisted is given in the following table.

Table 4.1. Category-wise number of beneficiaries (1998-99 to 2000-2001)

Year	*SC*	*BC*	*General*	*Total*
1998-1999	1115	829	42	1986
1999-2000	1169	863	10	2042
2000-2001	1401	1104	15	2520
Total	3685 (56.2)	2796 (42.8)	67 (1.0)	6548 (100.0)

Figures in parentheses denote percentages

The data in Table 4.1 reveal that total beneficiaries assisted 3685 (56.2%) were SC beneficiaries and 2796 (42.8%) were BC beneficiaries. The remaining 67 (1%) were general category's beneficiaries who were living below poverty line.

2. BALIKA SAMRIDHI YOJANA

'Balika Samridhi Yojana', an integrated scheme to raise the status of girl child was formally launched by the Prime Minister in Nilothi village, Delhi on Gandhi Jayanti, 2nd October, 1997 by distributing a grant of Rs. 500/- to the mother of a few girl children born on or after 15.8.1997 in families below poverty line.

The new integrated scheme to raise the status of the girl-child—Balika Samridhi Yojana has been prepared on the basis of consultations with the State Governments who have been implementing similar programmes. This is the first programmatic initiative of the Government of India at the national (all India) level to address in a holistic manner the problem of female foeticide and infanticide and the overall lower status of the girl child.

Objectives of the Balika Samridhi Yojana

The specific objectives of the programme are:

1. To change family and community attitude to the girl child at birth and towards her mother.

2. To improve enrolment and retention of girl children in schools.
3. To raise the age at marriage of girls.
4. To enable girls to undertake higher studies or income generating activities.

The other objectives which would be indirectly served are:

1. Ensuring survival of the girl child.
2. Serving as a disincentive for female foeticide and infanticide.
3. Reducing the incidence of a girl child labour within and outside the household.
4. Reinforcing positive perceptions of the girl child; changing social attitudes and behavioural practices towards her.
5. Raising the oversall status of the girl child; enhancing the self-esteem and self-confidence of the girl child.
6. Correcting the demographic imbalance due to declining ratio of females to males and promoting demographic transition by reducing the birth rate.

Assistance Provided

Under the programme, the mother of a girl child born on or after 15th August, 1997 in a family living below poverty line is given a grant of Rs. 500/-. The benefits and means of delivery have been redesigned in the current financial year i.e. 2000. The post-delivery grant of Rs. 500/- per girl child is deposited in bank account in the name of the girl child or in a post office if there is no bank nearby. In the same account will be deposited annual scholarships ranging from Rs. 300 for Class I to Rs. 1,000 for Class X when the girl starts going to school. The matured value of the deposits (alongwith interest) will be repayable to the girl on her attaining the age of 18 years and having remained unmarried till then.

Beneficiaries of the Balika Samridhi Yojana

The benefits of programme accrue to:

a) Girl child born in families below poverty line and are in the list of identified families available with DRDA's.

b) Upto two girl children in each below poverty line family irrespective of the number of children in the family.

Procedure for applying/obtaining the Benefit

It is the duty of AWW in rural area to identify the pregnant women through house to house survey and educate them about benefits and objectives of programme.

The application forms are collected from anganwadi centres in rural areas and the information duly filled in the forms and approved or ratified by Anganwadi worker, Sarpanch and the Gram Panchayat. The information is further certified by the Child Development Project Officer. The post-delivery grant of Rs. 500 is deposited in the name of girl child in bank or post office and the Pass Book is given to the mother of girl child.

Organizational Setup

To study the organizational setup, the authorities and roles at different levels of administration was assessed, the findings are presented in Fig. 4.2.

The scheme is being implemented both in urban and rural areas at Central level. It can be observed that at the Central level the Secretary, Department of Women and Child Development, New Delhi is the overall incharge of Balika Samridhi Yojana. At the State level, the Director, Women and Child Development Department, Haryana is responsible for planning at various levels. At the District level, Programme Officer is authority for supervision and guidance of the activities of block and village level. At the Block level, Child Development Project Officer is incharge and is responsible for the group activities. At the village level, Anganwadi Supervisor and Anganwadi workers are

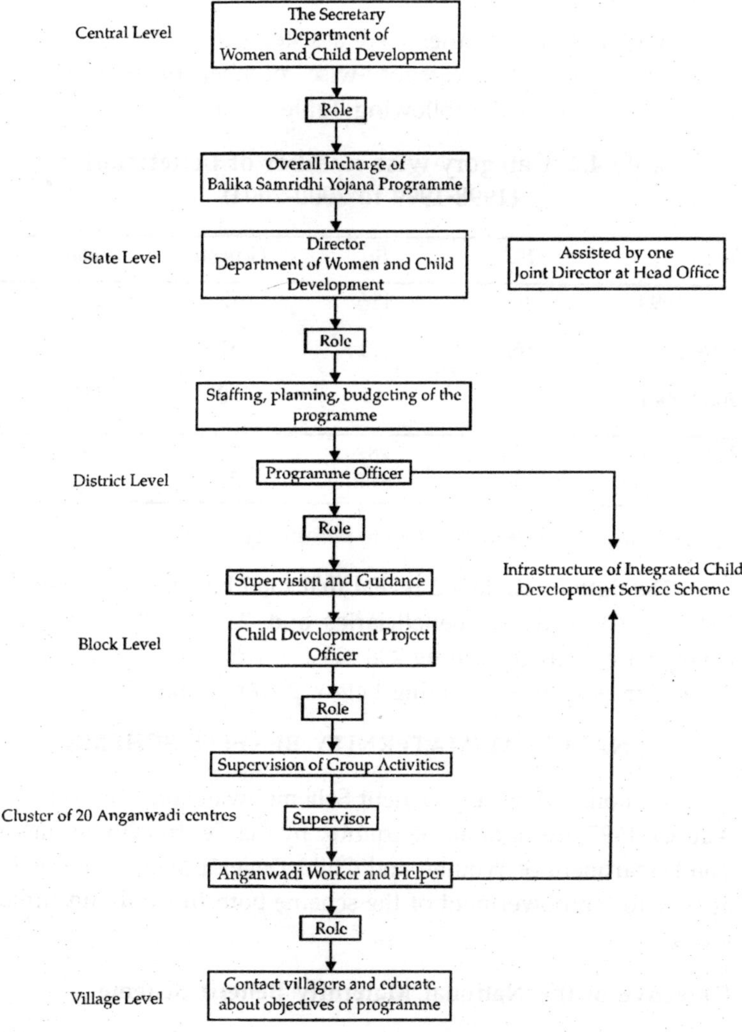

Fig. 4.2 Organisational Setup of 'Balika Samridhi Yojana' programme

incharge. Their job is to contact villagers frequently, maintenance of registers and educate beneficiaries about objectives of programme.

Number of beneficiaries in the year 1998-99 to 2000-2001 in Distt. Fatehabad

In all, 824 beneficiaries were assisted during the year 1998-99 to 2000-2001. The category-wise number of beneficiaries assisted is given in the following Table:

Table 4.2. Category-wise number of beneficiaries (1998-1999 to 2000-2001)

Year	*SC*	*BC*	*General*	*Total*
1998-1999	85	116	77	278
1999-2000	162	121	81	364
2000-2001	87	45	50	182
Total	334 (40.6)	282 (34.2)	208 (25.2)	824 (100.00)

Note: Figures in parentheses denote percentages.

The data in Table 4.2 reveal that total beneficiaries assisted 334 (40.6%) were SC beneficiaries and 282 (34.2%) were BC beneficiaries. The remaining 208 (25.2%) were general category's beneficiaries who were living below poverty line.

3. NATIONAL MATERNITY BENEFIT SCHEME

'National Maternity Benefit Scheme' was launched on 15th August, 1995 throughout the country by the Central Government. The Department of Women and Child Development is the nodal agency for empowerment of the scheme both in rural and urban areas.

Objective of the National Maternity Benefit Scheme

The main objective of this programme is to raise the nutritional status of the pregnant women.

Assistance provided by National Maternity Benefit Scheme

Under this programme, initially, an amount of Rs. 300/- was given to pregnant women in between 7-9 months of pregnancy for her improved nutrition. Since 1st August 1998, the amount has been increased from Rs. 300/- to Rs. 500/-.

Beneficiaries

The benefits of the programme accrue to:

a) Women belonging to families below poverty line and are in the list of identified families available with DRDAs.

b) The age of pregnant women must be above 19 years.

c) The benefit is availed by the pregnant women 8 to 12 weeks before the birth of child.

Procedure for applying/obtaining the benefit

It is the duty of Anganwadi worker in rural area to identify the pregnant women through house to house survey and monitor it till the birth of child. The forms are given to mother/father/guardian for availing benefit of Rs. 500/- for nutrition of mother. The required information are filled in the form and the certificate of pregnancy is issued by A.N.M. in the village and other information in the form of is certified by Gram Panchayat and given to A.W.W. in rural areas and forwarded to Supervisor (ICDS) for release of funds and form is collected from Medical Officer in urban areas.

Organizational Setup

To study the organizational setup, the authorities and roles at different levels of administration was assessed, the findings are presented in Fig. 4.3.

The scheme is being implemented both in urban and rural areas at Central level. It can be observed that at the Central level the Secretary, Department of Women and Child Development, New Delhi is the overall Incharge of National Maternity Benefit Scheme. At the State level, the Director, Women and Child Development, Haryana is responsible for planning at various levels. At the District level, Programme Officer is authority for supervision and guidance of the activities of block and village

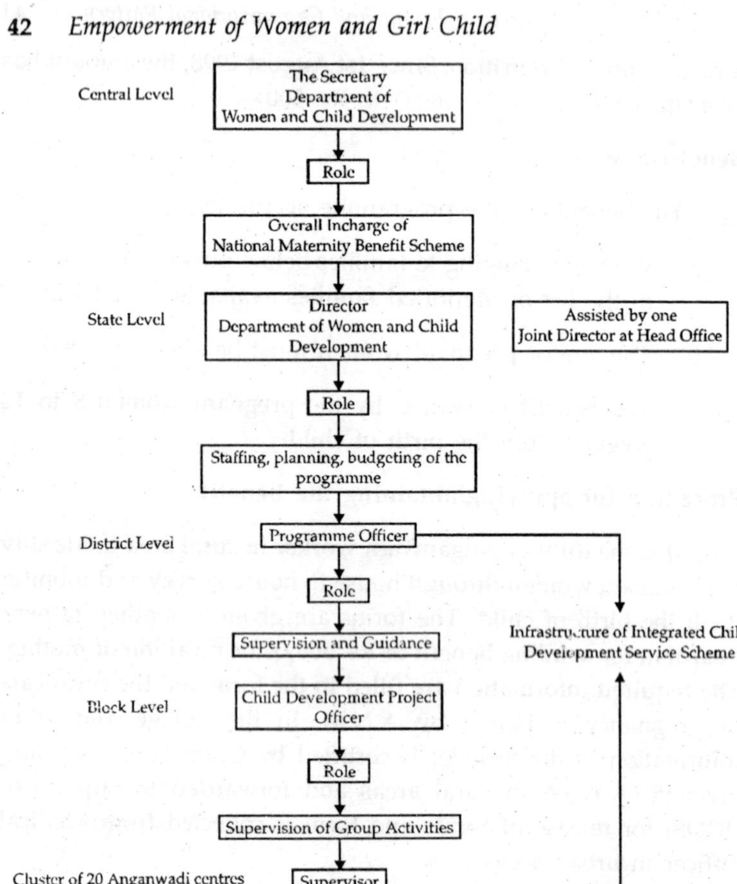

Fig. 4.3 Organisational setup of 'National Maternity Benefit Scheme'

level. At the Block level, Child Development Project Officer is incharge and is responsible for the group activities. At the village level, Anganwadi Supervisor and Anganwadi workers are incharge. Their job is to contact villagers frequently, maintenance of registers and educate beneficiaries about objectives of programme.

Number of beneficiaries benefitted during the year 1998-99 to 2000-2001 in Distt. Fatehabad

In all, 1105 beneficiaries were assisted during the eyar 1998-99 to 2000-2001. The category-wise number of beneficiaries assisted is given in the following table:

Table 4.3. Category-wise number of beneficiaries (1998-1999 to 2000-2001)

Year	*SC*	*BC*	*General*	*Total*
1998-1999	204	261	171	636
1999-2000	106	73	55	234
2000-2001	163	53	19	235
Total	473 (42.9)	387 (35.0)	245 (22.1)	1105 (100.0)

Note: Figures in parentheses denote percentages.

The data in Table 4.3 reveal that total beneficiaries assisted 473 (42.9%) were SC and 387 (35%) were from backward class. The remaining 245 (22.1%) were general category's beneficiaries who were living below poverty line.

All the three developmental programmes viz. ABAD, NMBS and BSY are run under ICDS. ABAD programme is the oldest programme amongst three. It was started in 1994 followed by NMBS in 1995 and BSY in 1997. The benefits of all the three developmental programmes are extended to families below poverty line. Organizational set up for all the three selected developmental programmes is fairly same. The only difference is that ABAD programme is implemented at State level whereas NMBS and BSY are implemented at central level. In all maximum beneficiaries during the year 1998-1999 to 2000-2001 are assisted in ABAD programme i.e. 6548, followed by NMBS i.e. 1105 and BSY i.e. 824.

5

Results and Discussion

The findings of the study and discussion therein have been presented in this chapter. The results have been organized on the basis of the objectives for the purpose of drawing meaningful inferences:

PERSONAL PROFILE OF THE RESPONDENTS

With a view to have a clear demographic picture of the beneficiaries, information about their profile variables were collected. Details of the same are presented in Table 5.1.

Age

Age-wise distribution of the respondents in Table 5.1 shows that out of total sample, 77.8 per cent respondents were from the age group of 20-30 years and remaining 22.2 per cent respondents were found in the age group of 30-40 years.

Education

When education was taken into consideration, the data in this respect indicated that out of total respondents, majority of the respondents were illiterate (90.0%) followed by primary school (6.7%) and middle school (3.3%).

Caste

The data indicated that more than half of the respondents (52.2%) belonged to scheduled caste, followed by backward class (28.9%) and only 18.9 per cent belonged to general category.

Table 5.1. Profile of beneficiaries

Sr. No.	*Variables*	*ABAD*	*BSY*	*NMBS*	*Total*
	Socio-personal and economic variables				
1.	**Age**				
	Young	22 (73.3)	25 (83.3)	23 (76.7)	70 (77.8)
	Middle	8 (26.7)	5 (16.7)	7 (23.3)	20 (22.2)
2.	**Education**				
	Illiterate	28 (93.4)	26 (86.7)	27 (0.0)	61 (90.0)
	Primary	1 (3.3)	3 (10.0)	2 (6.7)	6 (6.7)
	Middle	1 (3.3)	1 (3.3)	1 (3.3)	3 (3.3)
3.	**Caste**				
	General	2 (6.7)	8 (26.7)	7 (23.3)	17 (18.9)
	BC	6 (20.0)	10 (33.3)	10 (33.3)	26 (28.9)
	SC	22 (73.3)	12 (40.0)	13 (43.4)	47 (52.2)
4.	**Family Type**				
	Nuclear	21 (70.0)	22 (73.3)	24 (80.0)	67 (74.5)
	Joint	9 (30.3)	8 (26.7)	6 (20.0)	23 (25.5)
5.	**Family Size**				
	Small	9 (30.0)	8 (26.7)	9 (30.0)	26 (28.9)
	Medium	17 (56.7)	19 (63.3)	16 (53.3)	52 (57.8)
	Large	4 (13.3)	3 (10.0)	5 (16.7)	12 (13.3)
6.	**Family Occupation**				
	Respondent				
	Labourer	20 (66.7)	18 (60.0)	16 (53.3)	54 (60.0)
	Housewife	10 (33.3)	12 (40.0)	14 (46.7)	36 (40.0)
	Husband				
	Labour	25 (83.3)	25 (83.3)	24 (80.0)	74 (82.2)
	Cultivation	5 (16.7)	5 (16.7)	6 (20.0)	16 (17.8)
7.	**Family Income**				
	Extremely Poor	5 (16.7)	7 (23.3)	8 (26.7)	20 (22.2)
	Very Poor	15 (50.0)	14 (46.7)	15 (50.0)	44 (48.9)
	Poor	10 (33.3)	9 (30.0)	7 (23.3)	26 (28.9)
8.	**Land Holding**				
	Landless	22 (73.3)	25 (83.3)	23 (76.7)	70 (77.8)
	Marginal	8 (26.7)	5 (16.7)	7 (23.3)	20 (22.2)
9.	**Nutritional Status**				
	Low Weight Normal	11 (36.7)	14 (46.7)	12 (40.0)	37 (41.1)
	Normal	13 (43.3)	12 (40.0)	12 (40.0)	37 (41.1)
	Obese Grade I	6 (20.0)	4 (13.3)	6 (20.0)	16 (17.8)

contd...

Sr. No.	*Variables*	*ABAD*	*BSY*	*NMBS*	*Total*
10.	**No. of Living Children**				
	1 to 2	13 (43.4)	11 (36.7)	10 (33.3)	34 (37.8)
	3	10 (33.3)	13 (43.3)	11 (36.7)	34 (37.8)
	More than 3	7 (23.3)	6 (20.0)	9 (30.0)	22 (24.4)
11.	**No. of Girl Children**				
	One	11 (36.7)	11 (36.7)	9 (30.0)	31 (34.4)
	Two	14 (46.7)	16 (53.3)	17 (56.7)	47 (52.3)
	Three	5 (16.6)	3 (10.0)	4 (13.3)	12 (13.3)
12.	**Social Participation**				
	No membership	22 (73.3)	27 (90.0)	26 (86.7)	75 (83.0)
	Member of an Organization	6 (20.0)	3 (10.0)	4 (13.3)	13 (14.4)
	Public Leader	2 (6.6)	0 (0.0)	0 (0.0)	2 (6.7)
	Communication Variables				
13.	**Mass Media Exposure**				
	Radio	7 (23.3)	5 (16.7)	7 (23.3)	19 (21.1)
	Television	2 (6.7)	1 (3.3)	2 (6.7)	5 (5.6)
	No exposure	21 (70.0)	24 (80.0)	21 (70.0)	66 (73.3)
14.	**Source of Information**				
	Low	7 (23.3)	19 (63.3)	12 (40.0)	38 (42.2)
	Medium	21 (70.0)	11 (36.7)	15 (50.0)	47 (52.2)
	High	2 (6.7)	0 (0.0)	3 (10.0)	5 (5.6)
15.	**Source of Motivation**				
	Low	19 (63.4)	21 (70.0)	18 (60.0)	58 (64.5)
	Medium	10 (33.3)	9 (30.0)	10 (33.3)	29 (32.2)
	High	1 (3.3)	0 (0.0)	2 (6.7)	3 (3.3)

Note: Figures in parentheses indicate percentage

Family Type

Distribution of respondents according to family type shows that majority of them had nuclear family (74.5%) followed by joint family (25.5%).

Family Size

The data revealed that 57.8% per cent respondents had medium size of family, 28.9 per cent had small size of family while only 13.3 per cent were having large family size.

Family Occupation

As regards occupation, 60 per cent of beneficiaries were found to be labourers followed by housewives (40%) whereas in case of husband's occupation, 82.2 per cent were labourers while only 17.8 per cent had cultivation as their occupation.

Family Income

The results revealed that the total annual family income in 48.9 per cent cases was between Rs. 10,000-20,000 followed by 28.9 per cent respondents who had family income between Rs. 20,000 to 25,000 whereas 22.2 per cent respondents had income upto Rs. 10,000 per annum.

Land Holding

The data indicated that majority (77.8%) of respondents had no land holding whereas 22.2 per cent had irrigated land upto 2.5 acres.

Nutritional Status of Mother

As regards nutritional status on the basis of Garrow's Index, 41.1 per cent beneficiaries were found to be in low weight normal category and an equal per cent in normal weight category whereas 17.8 per cent were found in category of obese grade I.

Number of Living Children per Beneficiary

The data revealed that 37.8 per cent beneficiaries had children upto 2 and an equal per cent had 3 children whereas 24.4 per cent had more than 3 children.

Number of Girl Children per Beneficiary

The result indicated that number of girl children was two in 52.3 per cent beneficiaries followed by 34.4 per cent who had I girl child while 13.3 per cent had 3 girl children.

Social Participation

Data in Table 5.1 further pointed out that 83.4 per cent respondents were not member of any organization. This was followed by member of an organization (14.4%) and public leader (2.2%).

COMMUNICATION VARIABLES

Mass Media Exposure

Considering the mass media exposure by the beneficiaries it was observed that radio was found to be used by 21.1 per cent beneficiaries followed by television (5.6%). However, 73.3 per cent beneficiaries had no exposure of mass media.

Source of Information

Regarding communication variables the Table 5.1 reveals that majority of ABAD beneficiaries (70.0%) had medium level of information source utilization whereas 63.3 per cent of BSY beneficiaries had low level of information source utilization. In aggregate also majority of the respondents (52.2%) had medium information source utilization followed by low level (42.2%).

Source of Motivation

As regards motivational source utilization, it is clear that majority of the respondents for all the three programmes had low level of motivational source utilization (63.3%, 70% and 60%) respectively.

It can be concluded from Table 5.1 that most of the beneficiaries were from young age group, illiterate, belonged to scheduled caste, having nuclear medium sized families, labourers, extremely poor and no land holding. They had no membership of any organization, no mass media exposure and medium level of information and low level of motivational source utilization.

Source of Information and Motivation used by Beneficiaries

Data in Table 5.2 reveal the source of information and motivation utilized by beneficiaries. It is clear from the Table that as regards localite source of information used by beneficiaries, 74.4 per cent got information from neighbour followed by friends (56.7%) whereas only 17.8 per cent got information from relatives.

Among the cosmopolite sources it was observed that majority (95.5%) got the information from Anganwadi workers, followed by Supervisor (81.1%) whereas 18.9 per cent got the same from Sarpanch. It can be concluded that the beneficiaries obtained information from more than one source.

As regards localite source of motivation 30 per cent of the respondents were motivated by their friends followed by 23.3 per cent who were motivated by their neighbours whereas 4.4 per cent were motivated by their relatives. Among the cosmopolite source, 55.6 per cent were motivated by Anganwadi workers followed by Supervisor (41.1%).

Table 5.2. Sources of Information and Motivation used by Beneficiaries

Sr. No.	*Variables*	*ABAD*	*BSY*	*NMBS*	*Total*
1.	**Sources of Information**				
	Localite				
	Relatives	4 (13.3)	6 (20.0)	6 (20.0)	16 (17.8)
	Neighbour	23 (76.6)	21 (70.0)	23 (76.6)	67 (74.5)
	Friends	19 (63.3)	15 (50.0)	17 (56.7)	51 (56.7)
	Sarpanch	5 (16.6)	7 (23.3)	5 (16.6)	17 (18.9)
	Cosmopolite				
	Programme Officer (ICDS)	0 (0.0)	0 (0.0)	0 (0.0)	0 (0.0)
	CDPO (ICDS)	0 (0.0)	0 (0.0)	0 (0.0)	0 (0.0)
	Supervisor (ICDS)	25 (83.3)	30 (76.7)	25 (83.3)	73 (81.1)
	AWW	30 (100.0)	28 (93.3)	28 (93.3)	86 (95.5)
	Bank Officials	0 (0.0)	0 (0.0)	0 (0.0)	0 (0.0)
2.	**Sources of Motivation**				
	Localite				
	Relatives	2 (6.6)	1 (3.3)	1 (3.3)	4 (4.4)
	Neighbour	9 (30.0)	5 (16.7)	7 (23.3)	21 (23.3)
	Friends	11 (36.6)	7 (23.3)	9 (30.0)	27 (30.0)
	Sarpanch	0 (0.0)	0 (0.0)	0 (0.0)	0 (0.0)
	Cosmopolite				
	Programme Officer (ICDS)	0 (0.0)	0 (0.0)	0 (0.0)	0 (0.0)
	CDPO (ICDS)	0 (0.0)	0 (0.0)	0 (0.0)	0 (0.0)
	Supervisor (ICDS)	13 (43.3)	11 (36.7)	13 (43.3)	37 (41.1)
	AWW	18 (60.0)	15 (50.0)	17 (56.7)	50 (55.6)
	Bank Officials	0 (0.0)	0 (0.0)	0 (0.0)	0 (0.0)

Note: Figures in parentheses indicate percentage.

The preference to localite sources have been established by Sharma and Sharma (1998) as they revealed that neighbours were considered important sources of information followed by friends and relatives. Therefore, the neighbours and friends could be treated as important sources of information.

Among cosmopolite sources the ICDS functionaries at village level AWWs and Supervisors were playing an important role in motivating beneficiaries.

KNOWLEDGE OF BENEFICIARIES ABOUT DEVELOPMENTAL PROGRAMMES FOR EMPOWERMENT OF MOTHER AND GIRL CHILD

Knowledge of beneficiaries regarding different aspects of 'Apni Beti Apna Dhan' programme

Knowledge of the beneficiaries towards the programme was measured with the help of structured knowledge inventory. The findings presented in Table 5.3 reveal that 43.3 per cent beneficiaries had partial knowledge regarding starting of programme whereas 56.7 per cent of the respondents had complete knowledge regarding target beneficiaries of the programme. Majority of the beneficiaries (66.7%) were having partial knowledge regarding benefit given to mother whereas 43.3 per cent had complete knowledge as regards benefit given to girl child. Regarding collection of form, 86.7 per cent had complete knowledge followed by 73.3 per cent beneficiaries who had complete knowledge as regards distribution of benefit of 'Apni Beti Apna Dhan' programme.

Knowledge of the beneficiaries regarding different aspects of Balika Samridhi Yojana programme

Data furnished in Table 5.4 reveal the knowledge of the beneficiaries regarding different aspects of 'BSY' programme. It is evident from the data that 43.3 per cent of the beneficiaries had partial knowledge regarding starting of programme as well as target beneficiaries and benefit given to mother. Half of the beneficiaries (50.0%) had no knowledge regarding benefit given to girl child as well as depositing of annual scholarship in the account of girl child. Whereas majority of beneficiaries (80.0%) were having complete knowledge regarding collection of form followed by 56.7 per cent of beneficiaries who had partial knowledge regarding maturity of deposit of 'BSY' programme.

Table 5.3. Knowledge of the beneficiaries regarding different aspects of 'Apni Beti Apna Dhan' programme

N=30

Sr. No.	*Aspects*	*Frequency*	*Percentage*
1.	**Starting of Programme**		
	Nil knowledge	8	26.7
	Partial knowledge	13	43.3
	Complete knowledge	9	30.0
2.	**Target beneficiaries**		
	Nil knowledge	7	23.3
	Partial knowledge	6	20.0
	Complete knowledge	17	56.7
3.	**Benefit given to mother**		
	Nil to knowledge	1	3.3
	Partial knowledge	20	66.7
	Complete knowledge	9	30.0
4.	**Benefit given to girl child**		
	Nil knowledge	5	16.7
	Partial knowledge	12	40.0
	Complete knowledge	13	43.3
5.	**Collection of form**		
	Nil knowledge	0	0
	Partial knowledge	4	13.3
	Complete knowledge	26	86.7
6.	**Distribution of benefit**		
	Nil knowledge	3	10.0
	Partial knowledge	5	16.7
	Complete knowledge	22	73.3

Table 5.4 Knowledge of the beneficiaries regarding different aspects of 'Balika Samridhi Yojana' programme

N=30

Sr. No.	*Aspects*	*Frequency*	*Percentage*
1.	**Starting of Programme**		
	Nil knowledge	9	30.0
	Partial knowledge	13	43.3
	Complete knowledge	8	26.7
2.	**Target beneficiaries**		
	Nil knowledge	10	33.3
	Partial knowledge	13	43.4
	Complete knowledge	7	23.3
3.	**Benefit given to mother**		
	Nil knowledge	5	16.7
	Partial knowledge	13	43.3
	Complete knowledge	12	40.0
4.	**Benefit given to girl child**		
	Nil knowledge	15	50.0
	Partial knowledge	9	30.0
	Complete knowledge	6	20.0
5.	**Collection form**		
	Nil knowledge	2	7.7
	Partial knowledge	4	13.3
	Complete knowledge	24	80.0
6.	**Depositing of annual scholarship in the account of girl child**		
	Nil knowledge	15	50.0
	Partial knowledge	9	30.0
	Complete knowledge	6	20.0
7.	**Maturity of deposit**		
	Nil knowledge	6	20.0
	Partial knowledge	17	56.7
	Complete knowledge	7	23.3

Knowledge of the beneficiaries regarding different aspects of 'NMBS' programme

Table 5.5 depicts the knowledge of the beneficiaries regarding different aspects of 'NMBS' programme. A perusal of data reveals that 46.6 per cent of beneficiaries were having complete knowledge regarding target beneficiaries of the programme as well as partial knowledge of age limit of pregnant women. Majority of the beneficiaries had complete knowledge regarding benefit given to mother (73.4%) and collection of form (83.3%). Further, 33.3 per cent of beneficiaries were having complete knowledge regarding issue of certificate of pregnancy as well as information in the form to be certified by village Panchayat. However, very few beneficiaries had partial knowledge regarding duration of availing benefit (13.3%) of 'NMBS' programme.

Extent of knowledge of beneficiaries regarding development programmes for empowerment of mother and girl child

Table 5.6 and Fig. 5.1 and 5.2 show the categories of the respondents established on the basis of extent of knowledge of beneficiaries regarding development programmes. It can be observed that as regards 'ABAD' programme, half of the beneficiaries had high knowledge followed by medium knowledge (43.3%) and low knowledge (6.7%). Regarding 'BSY' programme, 50 per cent of beneficiaries had medium knowledge whereas 36.7 per cent had low knowledge whereas 43.4 per cent of the beneficiaries of 'NMBS' programme had medium knowledge followed by high knowledge (33.3%) and low knowledge (23.3%).

Table 5.5. Knowledge of the beneficiaries regarding different aspects of 'National Maternity Benefit Scheme' programme

N=30

Sr. No.	*Aspects*	*Frequency*	*Percentage*
1.	**Target beneficiaries**		
	Nil knowledge	8	26.7
	Partial knowledge	8	26.7
	Complete knowledge	14	46.6

contd...

Sr. No.	*Aspects*	*Frequency*	*Percentage*
2.	**Age limit of pregnant woman**		
	Nil knowledge	5	16.7
	Partial knowledge	14	46.6
	Complete knowledge	11	36.7
3.	**Benefit given to mother**		
	Nil knowledge	4	13.3
	Partial knowledge	4	13.3
	Complete knowledge	22	73.4
4.	**Duration for availing benefit**		
	Nil knowledge	18	60.0
	Partial knowledge	4	13.3
	Complete knowledge	8	26.7
5.	**Collection of form**		
	Nil knowledge	2	6.7
	Partial knowledge	3	10.0
	Complete knowledge	25	83.3
6.	**Issue of certificate of pregnancy**		
	Nil knowledge	11	36.7
	Partial knowledge	9	30.0
	Complete knowledge	10	33.3
7.	**Information in the form to be certified by Village Panchayat**		
	Nil knowledge	13	43.4
	Partial knowledge	7	23.3
	Complete knowledge	10	33.3

Table 5.6. Extent of knowledge of beneficiaries regarding developmental programme for empowerment of mother and girl child

Category	*ABAD*	*BSY*	*NMBS*	*Total*
High	15 (50.0)	4 (13.3)	10 (33.3)	29 (32.2)
Medium	13 (43.3)	15 (50.0)	13 (43.4)	41 (45.6)
Low	2 (6.7)	11 (36.7)	7 (23.3)	20 (22.2)

Note: Figures in parentheses indicate percentage

Therefore, almost half of the beneficiaries (45.6%) were

Fig. 5.1 Extent of knowledge of beneficiaires regarding development programme for empowerment of mother and girl child

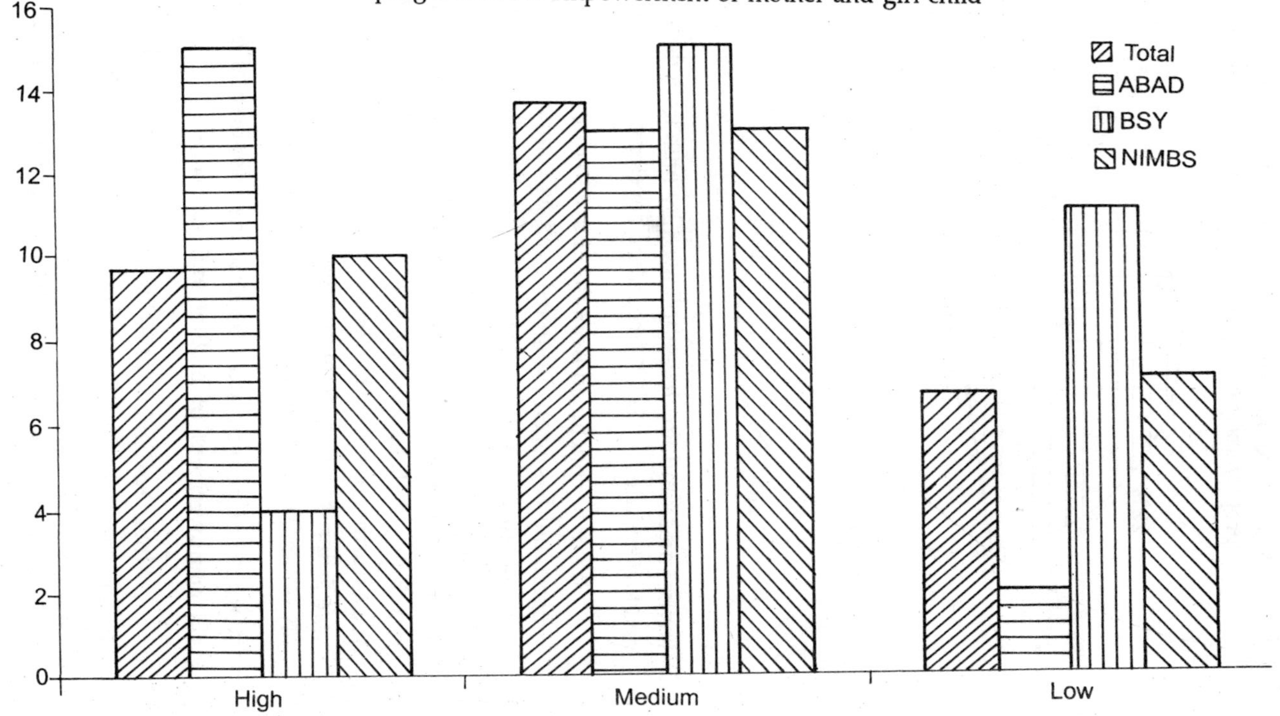

Fig. 5.2 Extent of knowledge of beneficiaires regarding development programme for empowerment of mother and girl child

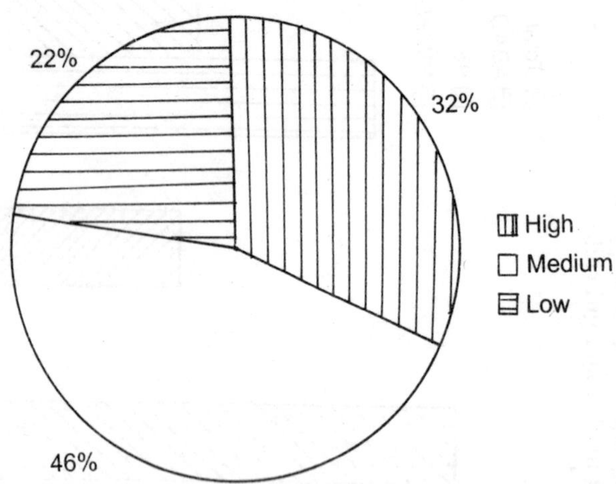

having medium knowledge followed by high knowledge (32.2%) and low knowledge (22.2%) regarding developmental programmes.

It can be concluded from the above findings that the 'ABAD' programme has been promoted well as compared to 'BSY' and 'NMBS' programme as half of the beneficiaries had high knowledge. Most of the beneficiaries were not aware or clear about Government's role but beneficiaries knowledge about health was better and other involvement raised image in family. It was further observed that beneficiaries were aware of availability of existing services. Similar views were shared by Narayanan (1989) and Padmanabhan *et al.* (1989).

Attitude of beneficiaries towards developmental programmes for empowerment of mother and girl child

Attitude of beneficiaries towards developmental programmes is depicted in Table 5.7 and Fig. 5.3 and 5.4. Results revealed that half of the beneficiaries (50.7%) had favourable attitude whereas only 3.3 per cent beneficiaries had strongly unfavourable attitude towards 'ABAD' programme. As regards 'BSY' programme 40 per cent were having neutral attitude followed by favourable (26.7%) and unfavourable attitude (20.0%). However, 40 per cent beneficiaries had favourable attitude and 16.6 per cent beneficiaries were having unfavourable attitude towards 'NMBS' programme.

Table 5.7. Attitude of beneficiaries towards developmental programmes for empowerment of mother and girl child

Category	*ABAD*	*BSY*	*NMBS*	*Total*
Strongly favourable	2 (7.7)	3 (10.0)	2 (6.7)	7 (7.8)
Favourable	15 (50.7)	8 (26.7)	12 (40.0)	35 (8.9)
Neutral	7 (22.5)	12 (40.0)	9 (30.0)	28 (31.1)
Unfavourable	5 (15.8)	6 (20.0)	5 (16.6)	16 (17.8)
Strongly unfavourable	1 (3.3)	1 (3.3)	2 (6.7)	4 (4.4)

Note: Figures in parentheses indicate percentage

Therefore, 38.9 per cent beneficiaries had favourable attitude followed by neutral attitude (31.1%) and unfavourable attitude (17.8%) towards developmental programmes. Aforesaid findings are in conformity with the results revealed by Kumar and Ramaiah (1992) as beneficiaries had favourable attitude followed by medium and less favourable attitude. As beneficiaries were involved in developmental programme, it was likely to have favourable attitude.

UTILIZATION OF BENEFITS OF DEVELOPMENTAL PROGRAMMES FOR EMPOWERMENT OF MOTHER AND GIRL CHILD

Procedural aspects regarding utilization of benefits of developmental programmes for empowerment of mother and girl child

Table 5.8 depicts for procedural aspects regarding utilization of benefits of developmental programmes by beneficiaries. It is clear from the Table that as regards ABAD, majority (83.3%) said that they had availed the benefit of programme once followed by 16.7 per cent who availed the benefit twice. Under NMBS, 93.3 per cent had availed the benefit once followed by 6.7 per cent who

Fig. 5.3 Attitude of beneficiaries towards development programme for empowerment of mother and girl child

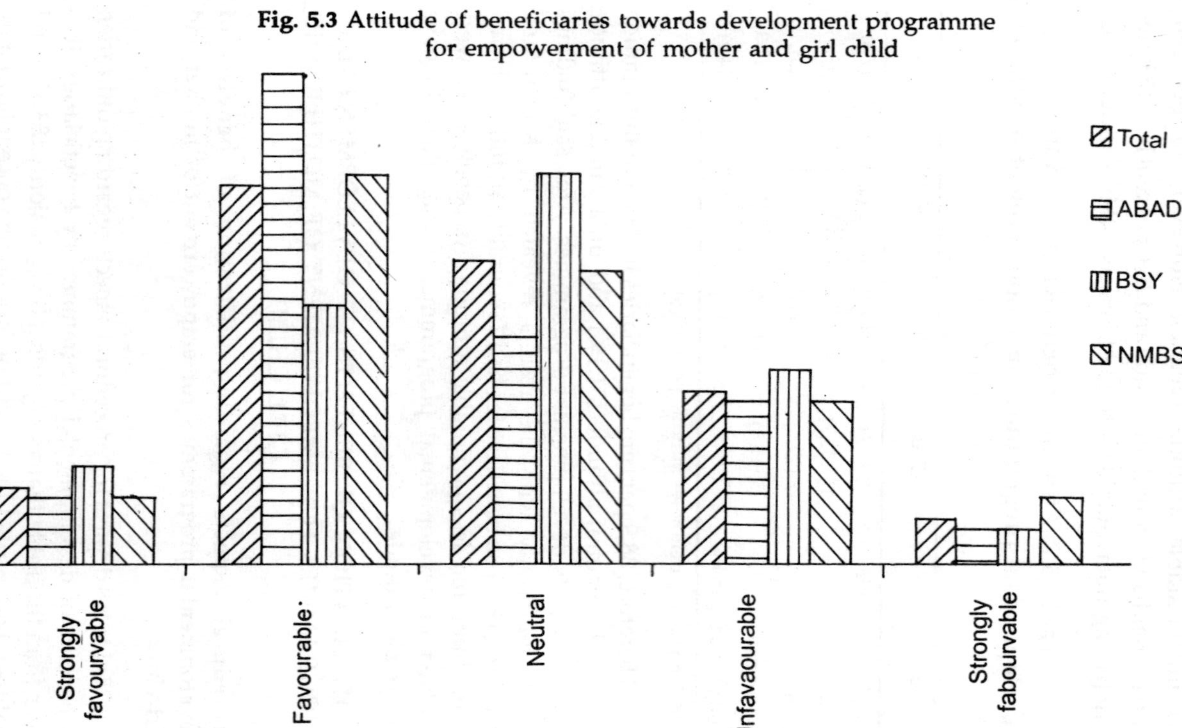

Fig. 5.4 Attitude of beneficiaries towards development programme for empowerment of mother and girl child

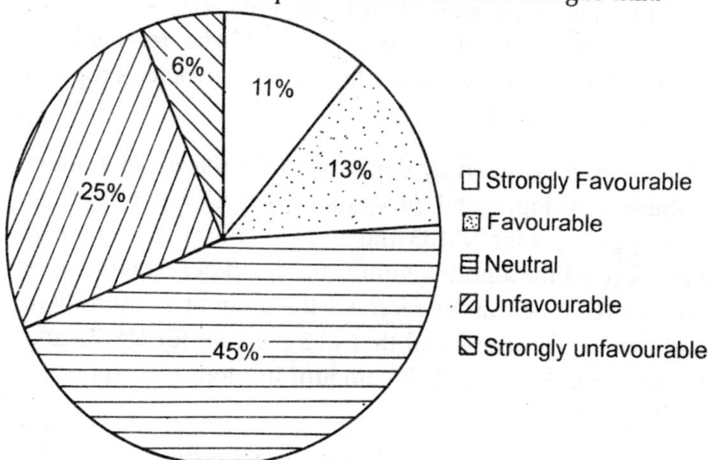

had availed the benefit twice. Under BSY, 100 per cent beneficiaries had availed the benefit once as the programme started just three years back i.e. in 1997.

Table 5.8. Procedural aspects regarding utilization of benefits of developmental programmes for empowerment of mother and girl child

Sr. No.	*Category*	*ABAD*	*BSY*	*NMBS*	*Total*
1.	**Programme benefit availed**				
	Once	25 (83.3)	30 (100.0)	28 (93.3)	83 (92.2)
	Twice	5 (16.7)	0 (0.0)	2 (6.7)	7 (7.8)
	More than two times	0 (0.0)	0 (0.0)	0 (0.0)	0 (0.0)
2.	**Amount obtained by mother and girl child in a family**				
	100%	5 (16.7)	11 (36.6)	16 (53.3)	32 (35.6)
	75-100%	9 (30.0)	12 (40.0)	14 (46.7)	35 (38.2)
	50-75%	16 (53.3)	2 (6.7)	0 (0.0)	18 (20.0)
	Less than 50%	0 (0.0%)	5 (16.7)	0 (0.0)	5 (5.5)
3.	**Time taken by department for release of amount**				
	Within stipulated period	19 (63.3)	21 (70)	17 (56.7)	57 (63.3)
	More than specified time	11 (365.6)	9 (30.0)	13 (43.3)	33 (36.7)

Figures in parentheses indicate percentage.

Further, Table reveals the amount obtained by mother and girl child in a family. It shows that in all, only 35.6 per cent got the 100% benefit followed by 38.2 per cent who received the amount between 75-100% and very few beneficiaries received less than 50 per cent benefit.

Regarding time taken by department for release of amount for all three developmental programme i.e. 63.3 per cent for ABAD, 56.7 per cent for NMBS and 70 per cent for BSY revealed that they received the amount within stipulated period while 36.6 per cent ABAD beneficiaries received the amount in more than specified time. Data also reveal that 43.3 per cent for NMBS and 30 per cent for BSY received the amount in more than specified time.

Extra expenditure incurred for obtaining benefit

The extra expenditure was incurred for completing the formalities to get the benefit. Due to their absence at the time of supervisor's visit to their village for making the payment, they had to collect their money from block headquarter and had to spend some money as fare. Data furnished in Table 5.9 reveal the extra expenditure incurred for obtaining benefit. It is evident from the data that under ABAD, 70 per cent beneficiaries did not spend any money for obtaining benefit while 30 per cent had to spend money for obtaining benefit. Under NMBS and BSY programmes also majority of the respondents (76.7% and 83.3% respectively) did not spend any money for obtaining benefit whereas 16.7 per cent of BSY beneficiaries had to spend some money for obtaining benefit.

Table 5.9. Extra expenditure incurred for obtaining benefit

Category	*ABAD*	*BSY*	*NMBS*	*Total*
Yes	9 (30.0)	5 (16.7)	7 (23.3)	21 (23.3)
No	21 (70.0)	25 (83.3)	23 (76.7)	69 (76.7)

Note: Figures in parentheses indicate percentage.

The Table thus clearly reveals that though in total majority (76.7%) beneficiaries did not have to spend any extra expenditure for obtaining benefit yet 23.3 per cent beneficiaries had to spend extra expenditure for obtaining benefit.

Views of beneficiaries regarding below poverty line (BPL) survey

The benefits of these developmental programmes are availed only by families below poverty line (BPL). The below poverty line survey is conducted for the identification of families below poverty line and the list of BPL families is available in DRDA office. Table 5.10 reveals the views of beneficiaries regarding below poverty line survey. The beneficiaries were inquired about the below poverty line survey conducted to identify the families and satisfaction with the BPL survey.

Table 5.10. Views of beneficiaries regarding below poverty line (BPL) survey

Category	*ABAD*	*BSY*	*NMBS*	*Total*
BPL survey conducted	24 (80.0)	25 (83.3)	27 (90.0)	76 (84.4)
BPL Survey not conducted	6 (20.0)	5 (16.7)	3 (10.0)	14 (15.6)
Satisfied with BPL survey	20 (83.3)	19 (76.0)	25 (92.6)	64 (84.2)
Not satisfied with BPL survey	4 (16.7)	6 (24.0)	2 (7.4)	12 (15.8)

Note: Figures in parentheses indicate percentage.

From the finding, it can be inferred that in total 84.4 per cent beneficiaries expressed their views that the BPL survey was conducted for identification of beneficiaries under developmental programmes. Further, the Table depicts that 15.8 per cent of the beneficiaries were not found to be satisfied with BPL survey while majority of the beneficiaries (84.2%) were satisfied with BPL survey. Findings of Gupta *et al.* (1979) also stated that a good number of beneficiaries were aware of services utilized by them and were satisfied. Thus, it can be concluded that majority of beneficiaries had a positive outlook regarding BPL survey.

Views of beneficiaries regarding the adequacy and existing arrangement of amount distribution

The views of beneficiaries regarding the adequacy and existing arrangement of amount distribution is depicted in Table 5.11. A cursory look at the Table pinpoints the fact that majority of the beneficiaries (72.2%) expressed their views that the amount provided was not adequate followed by 27.8 per cent beneficiaries who were reportedly satisfied with its adequacy.

Table 5.11 Views of beneficiaries regarding the adequacy and existing arrangement of amount distribution

Sr. No.	*Category*	*ABAD*	*BSY*	*NMBS*	*Total*
1.	**Regarding the adequacy**				
	Adequate	6 (20.0)	9 (30.0)	10 (33.3)	25 (27.8)
	Inadequate	24 (80.0)	21 (70.0)	20 (66.7)	65 (72.2)
2.	**Arrangement of amount distribution**				
	Satisfied	25 (83.3)	19 (63.3)	28 (93.3)	72 (80.0)
	Not satisfied	5 (16.6)	11 (36.7)	2 (6.7)	18 (20.0)

Note: Figures in parentheses indicate percentage.

Further, the Table reveals that 80 per cent of beneficiaries expressed satisfaction about existing arrangement of amount distribution whereas only 20 per cent beneficiaries were not satisfied with the existing arrangements.

Distribution of beneficiaries regarding health check up during pregnancy and their satisfaction about services provided at village level by Anganwadi centres

Data furnished in Table 5.12 depict the information about attending Anganwadi centres for health check-up during pregnancy. From the above Table, it will be observed that majority of the beneficiaries (80%) had attended the Anganwadi centres for health check-up during their pregnancy whereas 20 per cent beneficiaries did not attend the Anganwadi centres for health check-up.

Table 5.12 Distribution of beneficiaries regarding health check up during their pregnancy and their satisfaction about services provided at village level by Anganwadi centres

Sr. No.	*Category*	*ABAD*	*BSY*	*NMBS*	*Total*
1.	**Visit to Anganwadi centres**				
	Visit	23 (76.7)	21 (70.0)	28 (93.3)	72 (80.0)
	No visit	7 (23.3)	9 (30.0)	2 (6.7)	18 (20.0)
2.	**Satisfaction with services provided**				
	Satisfied	17 (73.9)	15 (71.4)	25 (89.3)	56 (77.8)
	Not satisfied	6 (26.1)	6 (28.6)	3 (10.7)	16 (22.2)

Note: Figures in parentheses indicate percentage

Further, the Table reveals that 77.8 per cent beneficiaries who had availed the health services were reportedly satisfied with the services provided in the Anganwadi centres while 22.2 per cent beneficiaries were not satisfied with the services provided therein.

Distribution of the sampled beneficiaries regarding motivation of family planning methods by village level ICDS functionaries

Data in Table 5.13 reveal that majority of beneficiaries (74.5%) were motivated for practising family planning methods by Anganwadi workers while 25.5 per cent beneficiaries reported that they were not motivated by any village level functionaries.

Table 5.13. Distribution of the sample beneficiaries regarding motivation of family planning methods by village level ICDS functionaries

Category	*ABAD*	*BSY*	*NMBS*	*Total*
Motivated	22 (73.3)	21 (70.0)	24 (80.0)	67 (74.5)
Not motivated	8 (26.7)	9 (30.0)	6 (20.0)	23 (25.5)

Note: Figures in parentheses indicate percentage.

Distribution of beneficiaries regarding visits of village level ICDS functionaries to the sampled beneficiaries

Data presented in Table 5.14 reveal the visits of village level ICDS functionaries to the sampled beneficiaries. It was reported by 81.1 per cent beneficiaries that village level ICDS functionaries had visited their homes after delivery of the child.

Table 5.14. Distribution of beneficiaries regarding visits of village level ICDS functionaries to the sampled beneficiaries

Sr. No.	*Category*	*ABAD*	*BSY*	*NMBS*	*Total*
1.	**Visit of village level ICDS functionaries to the sample beneficiaries**				
	Yes	27 (90.0)	21 (70.0)	25 (83.3)	73 (81.1)
	No	3 (10.0)	9 (30.0)	5 (16.7)	17 (18.9)
2.	**No. of visits of village level ICDS functionaries to house of beneficiaries**				
	Once	3 (10.0)	4 (13.3)	5 (16.7)	12 (13.3)
	2 times	3 (10.0)	9 (30.0)	6. (6.7)	18 (20.0)
	3 times	7 (23.3)	6 (20.0)	3 (10.0)	16 (17.7)
	4 times	14 (46.7)	2 (6.7)	11 (36.6)	27 (30.0)

Note: Figures in parentheses indicate percentage.

Regarding number of visits of village level ICDS functionaries to house of beneficiaries it was seen that 30 per cent of beneficiaries were visited 4 times, 20 per cent for 2 times followed by 3 times (17.7%) and once (13.3%). The remaining beneficiaries (18.9%) reported that no functionary of any department visited their houses. They collected the application forms as well as financial assistance from Anganwadi centres themselves.

Impact of utilization of programme benefits on empowerment of mother and girl child

Data related to impact of utilization of programme benefits on empowerment of mother and girl child are presented in Table 5.15 and Fig. 5.5 Results show that delaying the age at marriage

Table 5.15 Impact of utilization of programme benefits on empowerment of mother and girl child

Sr. No.	*Aspects*	*ABAD*	*SBY*	*NMBS*	*Total*	*Rank*
1.	Reduced mortality rate of girls	21 (70.0)	18 (60.0)	19 (63.3)	58 (64.4)	II
2.	Change in attitude of family towards mother and girl child	18 (60.0)	17 (56.6)	17 (56.6)	52 (57.8)	III
3.	To delay the age at marriage of girls atleast upto 18 years	22 (73.3)	25 (83.3)	20 (66.7)	67 (74.4)	I
4.	To bring down birth rate	14 (46.6)	16 (53.3)	14 (46.6)	44 (48.9)	IV
5.	In imparting education to girl child	8 (26.6)	21 (70.0)	9 (30.0)	38 (42.2)	VI
6.	In improving nutritional status of mother and girl child	17 (56.7)	9 (30.0)	16 (53.3)	42 (46.7)	V

Note: Figures in parentheses indicate percentage.

of girls atleast upto 18 years got I rank as the matured value was given to beneficiaries after 18 years and if the girl child in unmarried till then. This was followed by reduced mortality rate of girls. Next aspects which had impact of utilization of programme benefits were change in attitude of family towards mother and girl child, to bring down birth rate, improving nutritional status of mother and girl child and in imparting education to a girl child secured III, IV, V and VI rank, respectively.

Therefore, we can see that the utilization of programme benefits provide short-term empowerment for mother as the benefit availed by mother is utilized at that time only whereas it provides long-term empowerment for girl child as the benefit of girl child is mature when she attains the age of 18 years and remains unmarried till then.

Similar findings were reported by Mehendate *et al.* (1985) who concluded that ICDS had definite impact on the health and

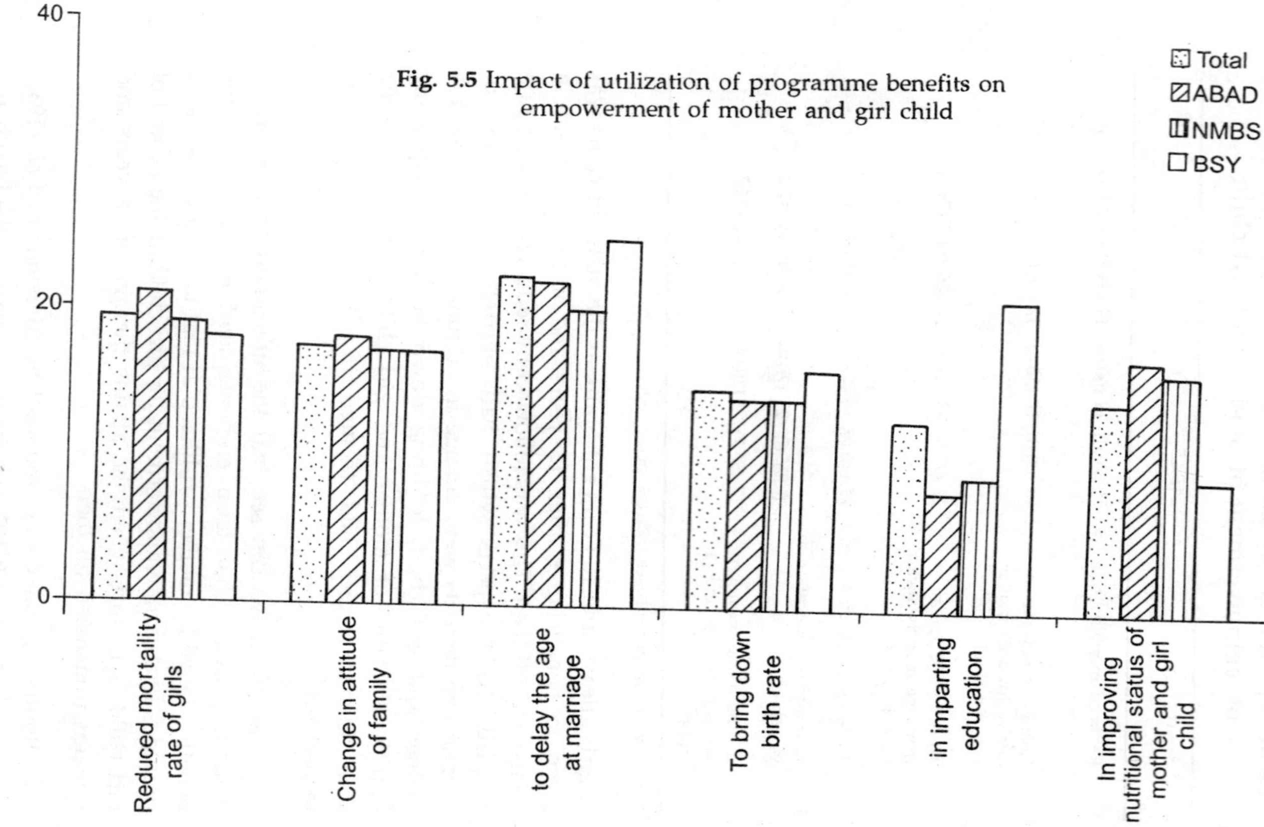

Fig. 5.5 Impact of utilization of programme benefits on empowerment of mother and girl child

nutritional status of children as the decrease in the incidence of malnutrition.

IMPACT OF DEVELOPMENTAL PROGRAMMES ON EMPOWERMENT OF MOTHER AND GIRL CHILD

Impact of 'Apni Beti Apna Dhan' programme on empowerment of mother and girl child

Impact of 'Apni Beti Apna Dhan' programme on empowerment of mother and girl child was computed through following formula:

$$I.A.I = \frac{\Sigma fi \times ci}{N \times X \times Y \times Z} \times 100$$

$$= \frac{336 \times 100}{30 \times 27} = \frac{3360}{81} = 41.5\%$$

The impact assessment index score reveals that 'Apni Beti Apna Dhan' programme has 41.5 per cent impact on empowerment of mother and girl child. In the present context, it can be interpreted that the programme has made in roads in improving the knowledge creating the favourable attitude and medium level of utilization of the programme.

Impact of 'Balika Samridhi Yojana' programme on empowerment of mother and girl child

Impact of 'Balika Samridhi Yojana' programme on empowerment of mother and girl child was computed through following formula:

$$I.A.I = \frac{\Sigma fi \times ci}{N \times X \times Y \times Z} \times 100$$

$$= \frac{244 \times 100}{30 \times 27} = \frac{2440}{81} = 30.1\%$$

The impact assessment index score reveals that the 'Balika Samridhi Yojana' programme has 30.1 per cent impact on empowerment of mother and girl child. In the present context, it can be interpreted that the programme has low impact upon the mother and girl child beneficiaries.

Impact of 'National Maternity Benefit Scheme' programme on empowerment of mother and girl child

Impact of 'National Maternity Benefit Scheme' programme on empowerment of mother and girl child was computed through following formula:

$$I.A.I = \frac{\sum fi \times ci}{N \times X \times Y \times Z} \times 100$$

$$= \frac{265 \times 100}{30 \times 27} = \frac{2650}{81} = 32.7\%$$

The impact assessment index score reveals that the 'National Maternity Benefit Scheme' programme has 32.7 per cent impact on empowerment of mother and girl child. In the present context, it can be interpreted that the programme has made in roads in

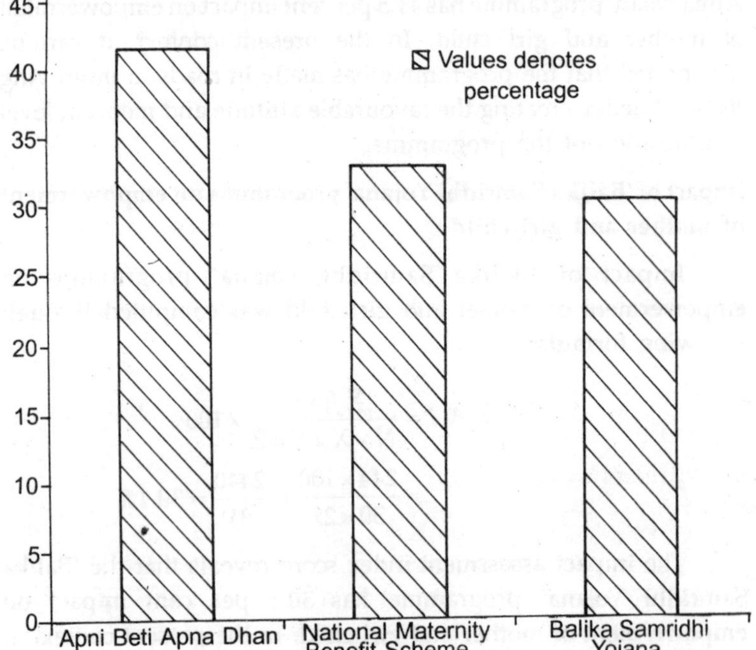

Fig. 5.6 Impact of development programme on empowerment of mother and girl child

improving the knowledge, creating favourable attitude and medium level of utilization of programme.

The impact of developmental programmes on empowerment of mother and girl child is shown in Fig. 5.6. It can be concluded that 'ABAD' programme had maximum impact on beneficiaries (41.5%) followed by NMBS (32.7%) and 'BSY' (30.1%). Thus, it clearly reveals that all the programmes could make considerable impact upon empowerment of mother and girl child and perceived improvement in the status of mother and girl child in family and society.

The findings are in line with findings of Sood (1994) who observed that impact of developmental programmes on women has not yet been augmenting. It is but essential that proper execution of projects is carried out thoroughly to achieve the developmental goals.

CONSTRAINTS FACED IN UTILIZATION OF BENEFITS OF THE DEVELOPMENTAL PROGRAMMES FOR EMPOWERMENT OF MOTHER AND GIRL CHILD

This section deals with the problems and constraints faced by beneficiaries in the utilization of the development programmes for empowerment of mother and girl child. These were assessed on developed schedule and the findings presented separately for each programme.

Constraints faced by beneficiaries in utilization of development programmes have been identified and categorized into Organizational, Economic, Educationl and Communicational and Socio-cultural constraints. The findings are presented hereafter.

Organizational constraints

Organizational constraints presented in Table 5.16 and Fig. 5.7 show that majority of the beneficiaries (83.4%) reported favouritism in selection of BPL families, favouritism in selection of beneficiaries (76.7%), lack of guidance of Gram Panchayat

Fig. 5.7 Organizational constraints faced by the beneficiaries in utilization of programme benefits

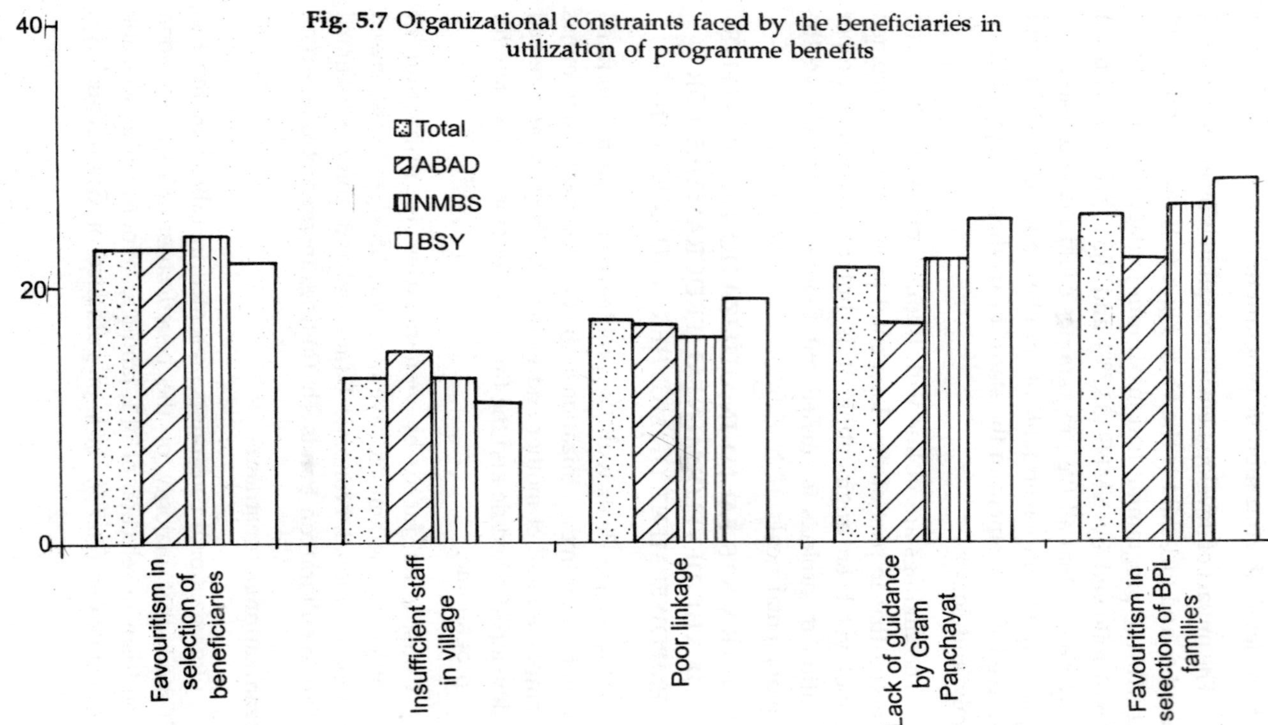

(71.1%), poor coordination and linkage between village staff and staff at district headquarter and insufficient staff in village i.e. AWW/Supervisor as the major constraints.

Similar results were revealed by Shekhar (1975) who reported a lack of coordination between health care delivery personnel and other development officials. Mehta (1971) also reported that the labourers, the poor, the non-agriculturists and the lower caste sub-groups seem to be least benefited from these programmes.

Table 5.16. Organizational constraints faced by the beneficiaries in utilization of programme benefits

Sr. No.	*Constraints*	*ABAD*	*SBY*	*NMBS*	*Total*	*Rank*
1.	Favouritism in selection of beneficiaries	23 (76.6)	22 (73.3)	24 (80.0)	69 (76.7)	II
2.	Insufficient staff in village	15 (50.0)	11 (36.7)	13 (43.3)	39 (43.3)	V
3.	Poor linkage	17 (56.6)	19 (63.3)	16 (53.3)	52 (57.8)	IV
4.	Lack of guidance by Gram Panchayat	17 (56.6)	25 (83.3)	22 (73.3)	64 (71.1)	III
5.	Favouritism in selection of BPL families	22 (73.3)	28 (93.3)	26 (86.7)	76 (83.4)	I

Note: Figures in parentheses indicate percentage.

Economic constraints

The findings presented in Table 5.17 and Fig. 5.8 reveal that 90 per cent beneficiaries reported delay in release of money as major constraint followed by lack of funds by Government (53.3%), amount not sufficient to meet nutritional requirement (47.8%), extra expenditure has to be paid for availing benefit (23.3%).

It can be inferred from the findings that faulty implementation and insufficient and irregular payment is hindering beneficiaries to utilize the benefits of development programmes. The findings of the study are in accordance with the early researches reported

Fig. 5.8 Economic constraints faced by the beneficiaries in utilization of programme benefits

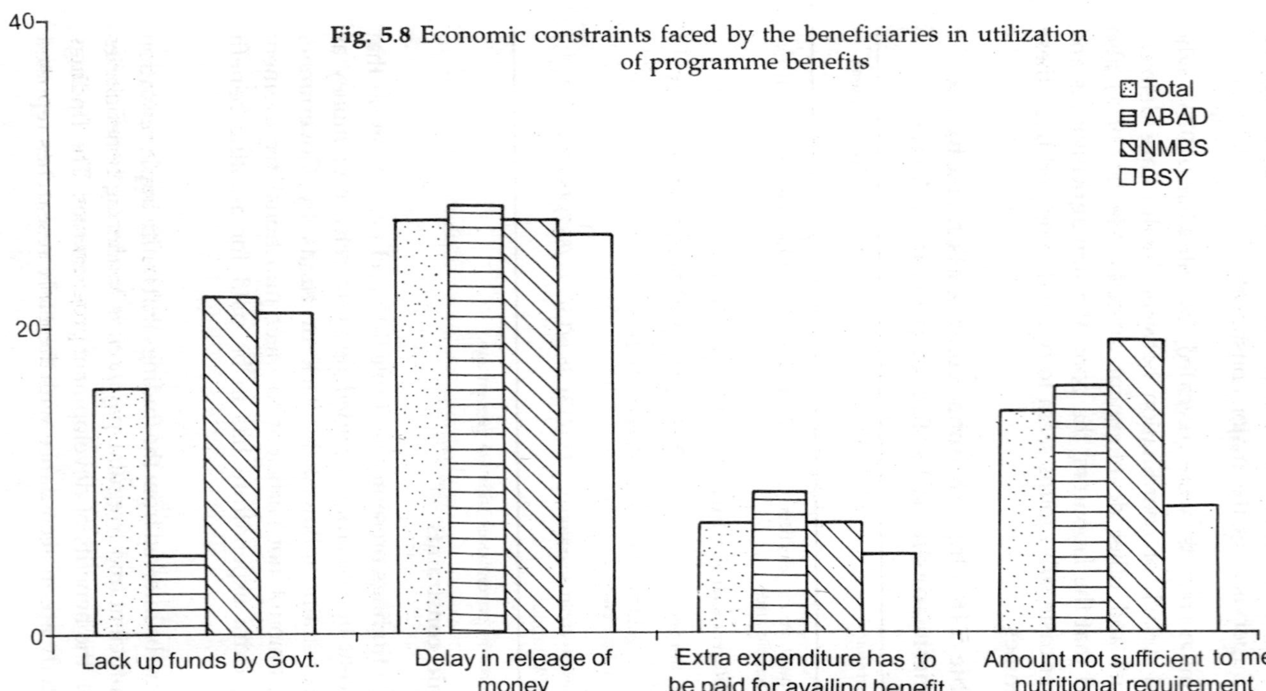

by Jorapur (1981) who asserted that the food distributed through Integrated Child Development Scheme was very meagre and the usual problem in the distribution of food were lack of sufficient food.

Table 5.17. Economic constraints faced by the beneficiaries in utilization of programme benefits

Sr. No.	*Constraints*	*ABAD*	*SBY*	*NMBS*	*Total*	*Rank*
1.	Lack of funds by Govt.	5 (16.6)	21 (70.0)	22 (73.3)	48 (53.3)	II
2.	Delay in release of money	28 (93.3)	26 (86.7)	27 (90.0)	81 (90.0)	I
3.	Extra expenditure has to be paid for availing benefit	9 (30.0)	5 (16.7)	7 (23.3)	21 (23.3)	IV
4.	Amount not sufficient to meet nutritional requirement	16 (53.3)	8 (26.7)	19 (63.3)	43 (47.8)	III

Note: Figures in parentheses indicate percentage

Educational and communicational constraints

Educational and communicational constraints presented in Table 5.18 and Fig. 5.9 show that majority of the beneficiaries (77.8%) reported lack of encouragement and motivation, lack of knowledge about objectives of programme (73.3%) lack of literature and timely guidance (68.8%), lack of knowledge about other schemes in operation (67.8%) and no proper extension staff to communicate (65.6%).

From the above cited result, it can be inferred that most of the beneficiaries felt the problem of lack of motivation, lack of guidance and knowledge. The results are in tune with early researches done by Dev and Lal (1989) who revealed that major constraints were inadequate knowledge of ICDS scheme, lack of proper training of Anganwadi worker, infrequent contacts with community due to lack of transport facilities and inadequate effort by ICDS functionaries to motivate beneficiaries.

Fig. 5.9 Educational and communicational constraints faced by the beneficiaries in utilization of programme benefits

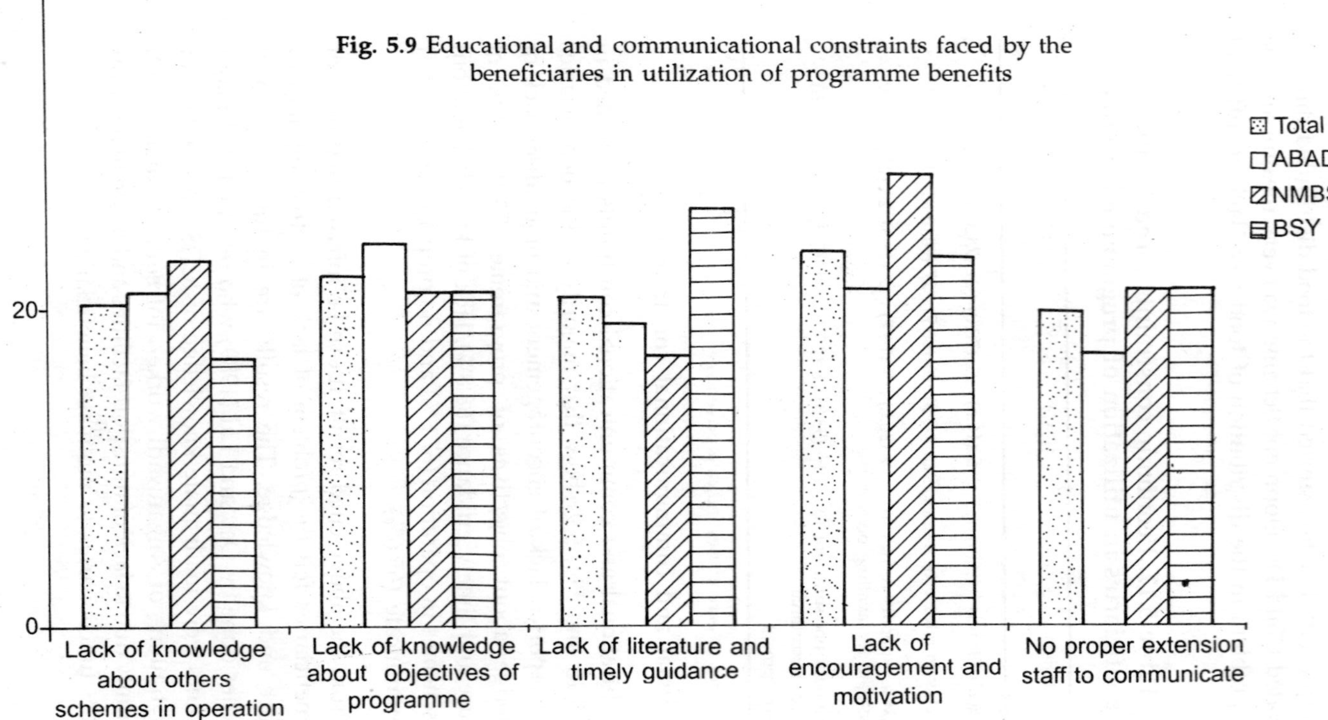

Table 5.18. Educational and communicational constraints faced by the beneficiaries in utilization of programme benefits

Sr. No.	*Constraints*	*ABAD*	*SBY*	*NMBS*	*Total*	*Rank*
1.	Lack of knowledge about other schemes in operation	21 (70.0)	17 (56.6)	23 (76.6)	61 (67.8)	IV
2.	Lack of knowledge about objectives of programme	24 (80.0)	21 (70.0)	21 (70.0)	66 (73.3)	II
3.	Lack of literature and timely guidance	19 (63.3)	26 (86.7)	17 (56.6)	62 (68.8)	III
4.	Lack of encouragement and motivation	21 (70.0)	23 (76.6)	28 (86.7)	70 (77.8)	I
5.	No proper extension staff to communicate	17 (56.6)	21 (70.0)	21 (70.0)	59 (65.6)	V

Note: Figures in parentheses indicate percentage.

Socio-cultural constraints

The findings presented in Table 5.19 and Fig. 5.10 reveal poor chance of mobility for mother (75.6%), lack of motivation from family and society as well as family responsibility and excessive burden of work at home and farm (66.7%), husband takes away the money (57.8%) and hindrance due to ill health (41.1%) are the constraints reported by most of the beneficiaries.

It can be inferred from the above results that it is the rural society, which hinders mother and girl child to utilize the benefits of developmental programme. The above cited results are in accordance with the previous researchers by Chakraborti *et al.* (1984) which revealed that a number of socio-psychological factors acting as barriers to adoption behaviour are joint family structure, lower sub-caste, illiteracy, lack of formal participation in village bodies, non-accessibility of media, lack of urban contact or occupational mobility, dearth of political knowledge, fatalism and lack of secular orientation.

Fig. 5.10 Socio-cultural constraints faced by the beneficiaries in utilization of programme benefits

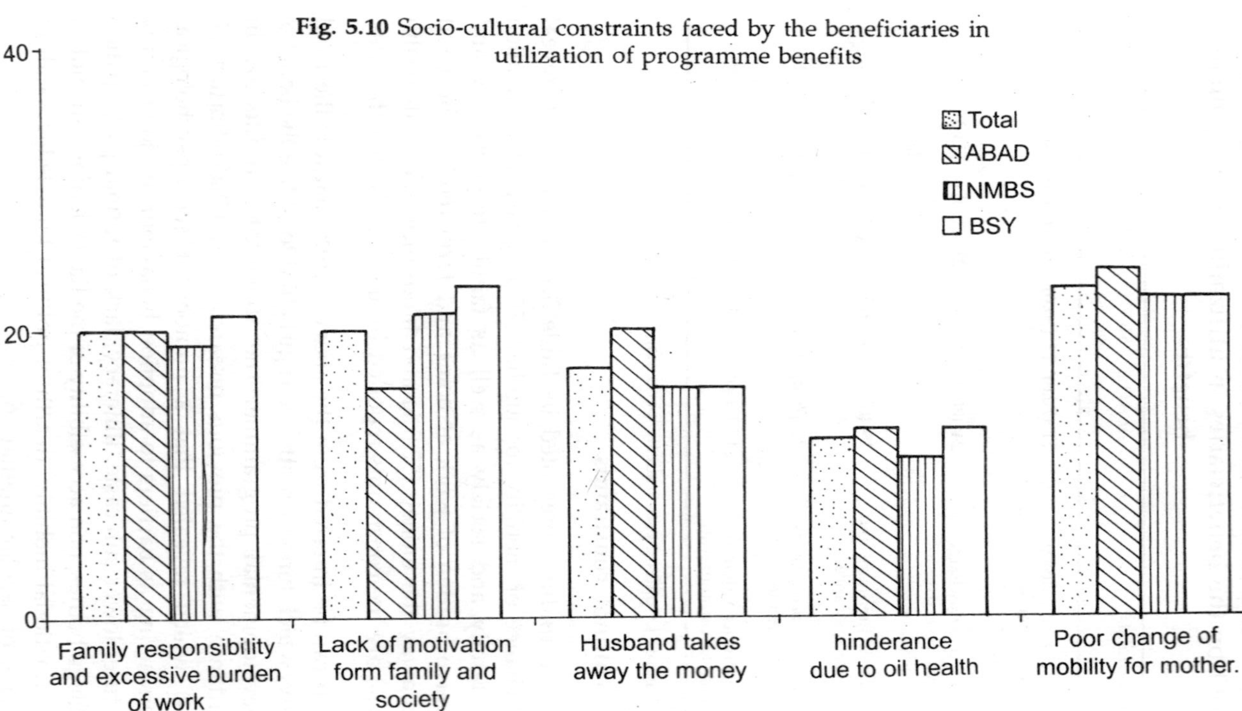

Table 5.19. Socio-cultural constraints faced by the beneficiaries in utilization of programme benefits

Sr. No.	*Constraints*	*ABAD*	*SBY*	*NMBS*	*Total*	*Rank*
1.	Family responsibility and excessive burden of work at home and farm	20 (66.6)	21 (70.0)	19 (63.3)	60 (66.7)	II
2.	Lack of motivation from family and society	16 (53.3)	23 (76.6)	21 (70.0)	60 (66.7)	II
3.	Husband takes away the money	20 (66.6)	16 (53.3)	16 (53.3)	52 (57.8)	III
4.	Hindrance due to ill health	13 (43.3)	13 (43.3)	11 (36.7)	37 (41.1)	IV
5.	Poor chance of mobility for mother	24 (80.0)	22 (73.3)	22 (73.3)	68 (75.6)	I

Note: Figures in parentheses indicate percentage.

6

Summary and Conclusion

The status of mother and girl child all over the world has lately become a focus of national and international concern, the culmination of growing concern for the girl child being subjected to inequality, disparity and neglect manifested in the decision to observe 1990 as the SAARC Year of the Girl Child and 2001 as Women's Empowerment Year.

Empowerment implies a process by which one's power of self organization is promoted and reinforced. The empowerred develops the capacity for self-reliance out-crossing the relationship of subordination on account of gender, social and economic status and the role in the family and society. It encompasses their ability to make choices, control resources and enjoy participatory relationship within family and community. India has been spending on the implementation of various developmental programmes with an objective of empowerment of mother and girl child. However, there is a need to study the organization of these programmes and to analyse the impact of these programmes. It is also important to isolate the constraints in utilization of the programme benefits. Hence, the present study was planned with a view to assess the impact of developmental programme on empowerment of mother and girl child with the following objectives:

(i) To assess the impact of developmental programmes on empowerment of mother and girl child.

(ii) To identify constraints faced by beneficiaries in utilization of developmental programmes for mother and girl child.

Methodology

The study was conducted in Fatehabad district of Haryana State by covering all the three programmes under ICDS for mother and girl child viz. ABAD, NMBS and BSY. A sample of 90 beneficiaries were selected randomly from three villages of Fatehabad district where all the three developmental programmes had been in operation for the last three years. To accomplish the specific laid down objectives of the study 4 dependent and 15 independent variables were included and were measured in accordance with the methodological procedure described under the chapter of methodology. A duly pretested schedule was used as tool for data collection. The data so collected were then analysed to draw the appropriate inferences by application of suitable statistical tests.

RESULT

Organizational pattern and impact of ABAD, NMBS and BSY

Organizational pattern and impact of ABAD

Organization set up of ABAD revealed that programme is operated at State level in both urban and rural areas. It can be observed that at State level the Director, Women and Child Department, Haryana was over all in-charge and responsible for planning, staffing, budgeting of the programme, who is assisted by one Joint Director, whereas at the district level Programme Officer is the authority for the same. At the Block level, Child Development Project Officer is responsible for implementation and supervision of ABAD programme. At a cluster of village level, supervisor is incharge. Where as the village level Anganwadi worker is responsible at village level and she is assisted by helper in organizing various services.

In all, 6548 beneficiaries were assisted during the year 1998-1999 to 2000-2001. Impact of ABAD was assessed by assessing the knowledge, attitude and utilization of programme benefits on an impact assessment index.

- It was found that most of the beneficiaries had high knowledge and favourable attitude.
- Majority of the beneficiaries availed the benefit of programme once and majority received the amount with in stipulated period.
- Majority of the beneficiaries were satisfied with the BPL Survey.
- The ABAD programme had medium level of impact i.e. 41.5 per cent.

Organizational pattern and impact of BSY

Organizational set up of BSY revealed that the programme is being implemented both in urban and rural areas at Central level. At Central level, the Secretary, Department of Women and Child Development, New Delhi is the over all incharge of BSY programme. At State level in both urban and rural areas it can be observed that the Director, Women and Child Department, Haryana was over all incharge and responsible for planning, staffing, budgeting of the programme, who is assisted by one Joint Director. Whereas at the district level, Programme Officer is the authority for the same. At the Block level, Child Development Project Officer is responsible for implementation and supervision of BSY programme. At a cluster of village level, Supervisor is incharge. Where as the village level Anganwadi worker is responsible and she is assisted by helper in organizing various services.

In all, 824 beneficiaries were assisted during the year 1998-1999 to 2000-2001.

Impact of BSY

- It was found that most of the beneficiaries had medium level of knowledge.
- It was observed that lesser number of beneficiaries had knowledge regarding all aspects of BSY.

- It was found that 40 per cent of the beneficiaries had neutral attitude, where as 26.7 per cent had favourable attitude towards BSY.
- In general, the utilization of benefits of BSY was low, as compared to ABAD and NMBS programme.
- None of the beneficiaries availed the benefit of BSY programme twice.
- The impact assessment index of 30.1 per cent revealed that BSY had low impact on mother and girl child.

Organizational pattern and impact of NMBS

Organizational set up of NMBS revealed that the programme is being implemented both in urban and rural areas at Central level. At Central level, the Secretary, Department of Women and Child Development, New Delhi is the over all incharge of NMBS programme. At State level in both urban and rural areas it can be observed that the Director, Women and Child Department, Haryana was over all incharge and responsible for planning, staffing, budgeting of the programme, who is assisted by one Joint Director. Whereas at the district level Programme Officer is the authority for the same. At the Block level, Child Development Project Officer is responsible for implementation and supervision of NMBS programme. At a cluster of village level, Supervisor is incharge. Where as at the village level Anganwadi worker is responsible and she is assisted by helper in organizing various services.

In all, 1105 beneficiaries were assisted during the year 1998-1999 to 2000-2001.

Impact of NMBS

- It was found that most of the beneficiaries had medium level of knowledge and favourable attitude.
- Majority of the beneficiaries availed the benefit of programme once.

- Very few beneficiaries received the benefit in more than specified time.
- Very few beneficiaries were not satisfied with the BPL survey.
- Majority of the beneficiaries were satisfied with the existing arrangement of amount distribution.
- The impact of NMBS was less as compared to ABAD programme.

Constraints faced in utilization of benefits of developmental programme for empowerment of mother and girl child

Organizational constraints

- Most of the beneficiaries reported favouritism in selection of BPL families as major constraint.
- 76.7 per cent of beneficiaries reported poor linkage and coordination between village staff and staff at district headquarter.
- Nearly half of the beneficiaries reported that there was insufficient staff in village.

Economic Constraints

- Most of the beneficiaries expressed delay in release of money as major constraint.
- 53.3 per cent beneficiaries reported that the amount was not sufficient to meet nutritional requirement.

Educational and Communicational constraints

- Most of the beneficiaries reported that there was lack of encouragement and motivation.
- 73.3 per cent of the beneficiaries expressed lack of knowledge about objectives of programme as an educational and communicational constraint.

- It was found that lack of literature and timely guidance and lack of knowledge about schemes in operation were the constraints faced by beneficiaries.
- It was observed that there was no proper extension staff to communicate.

Socio-cultural constraints

- Most of the beneficiaries reported poor chance of mobility for mother as major constraint.
- 66.7 per cent of the beneficiaries expressed family responsibility and excessive burden of work as well as lack of motivation from family and society—as socio-cultural constraint.
- It was found that hindrance due to ill health was the constraint faced by beneficiaries.

Conclusion

It can be concluded that ABAD, NMBS, and BSY are the developmental programmes which have been implemented for empowerment of mother and girl child. Though the organization and implementation of the programme has created improved knowledge and favourable attitude among mothers, yet the utilization of programme benefits has not been to a great extent. Beneficiaries faced substantial organizational, economic, socio-cultural, educational and communication constraints which hinder the utilization of programme benefits.

Suggestions

In view of the findings few suggestions are made for the better organization and implementation of developmental programmes for empowerment of mother and girl child which are as follows:

1. The findings reveal that there are very few schemes exclusively for mother and girl child. Therefore, more mother and girl child specific schemes should be started

keeping in mind the special needs of mother and girl child.

2. A proper and comprehensive below poverty line survey should be conducted to identify the deserving poor families. This would result in detecting the needy households, so that all people irrespective of caste and creed may get the benefit of the scheme.

3. The concerned authority should sanction and disburse the amount in stipulated period.

4. Frequent awareness programmes should be conducted to create awareness about developmental programmes operating for their benefit and also their objectives and procedural aspects.

5. Beneficiaries faced constraints such as no coordination and linkage between village staff and staff at district headquarters, lack of encouragement and motivation. Hence, the concerned authorities should be more cooperative and encouraging.

Views of CDPOs

The views of CDPO about the general functioning of developmental programmes for empowerment of mother and girl child and the constraints in smooth implementation are given in the following paragraphs.

The programmes are implemented by the staff of Integrated Child Development Services Programme at village/block level in rural areas. CDPO is the incharge of programme at block level in rural areas.

1. CDPO reported that the main aim of the development programmes related with mother and girl child is change in attitude of family towards mother and girl child.

2. CDPO reported that there is no separate staff provided under the programmes. The existing staff of Women and

Child Development Department i.e. Programme Officer at district level, CDPO at block level, Supervisor/AWW at village level were looking after these programmes. But CDPO felt that there was need for additional or separate staff for proper implementation of development programmes.

3. CDPO also reported that no separate household Survey (BPL) was conducted for identification of beneficiaries under the programme and the benefit of the programme was provided according to old BPL list. Therefore, proper identification of beneficiary for coverage under the programmes seemed to be lacking.

4. CDPO was of the view in regard to change in attitude of the family and society towards mother/girls, that there had been definite change in the attitude of the family and society due to social awareness and monetary gains and the girls are not considered a burden now.

5. Overall suggestions of the CDPOs were

   (i) Separate staff should be provided for these programmes.

   (ii) A proper and comprehensive BPL survey may be conducted to detect the deserving families.

Appendices

Appendix-I (a)

Impact Assessment Index of 'Apni Beti Apna Dhan' programme on empowerment of mother and girl child

Knowledge/ Utilization		*Attitude*		
		Favourable	*Somewhat favourable*	*Unfavourable*
		(3)	*(2)*	*(1)*
		fi×ci	fi×ci	fi×ci
High (3)	H	0×27	0×18	0×9
	M	11×18	3×12	0×6
	L	0×9	1×6	0×3
Medium (2)	H	0×18	0×12	1×6
	M	3×12	2×8	3×4
	L	2×6	0×4	2×2
Low (1)	H	0×9	0×6	0×3
	M	1×6	1×4	0×2
	L	0×3	0×2	0×1

H = High

M = Medium

L = Low

Appendix-I (b)

Impact Assessment Index of 'Balika Samridhi Yojana' programme on empowerment of mother and girl child

Knowledge/ Utilization		*Attitude*		
		Favourable (3)	*Somewhat favourable* (2)	*Unfavourable* (1)
		fi×ci	fi×ci	fi×ci
High (3)	H	0×27	0×18	0×9
	M	2×18	1×12	0×6
	L	0×9	1×6	0×3
Medium (2)	H	1×18	2×12	0×6
	M	5×12	4×8	1×4
	L	1×6	1×4	0×2
Low (1)	H	0×9	1×6	2×3
	M	2×6	2×4	3×2
	L	0×3	0×2	1×1

H = High

M = Medium

L = Low

Appendix-I (c)

Impact Assessment Index of 'National Maternity Benefit Scheme' programme on empowerment of mother and girl child

Knowledge/ Utilization		*Favourable* (3)	*Attitude Somewhat favourable* (2)	*Unfavourable* (1)
		fi×ci	fi×ci	fi×ci
High (3)	H	0×27	0×18	0×9
	M	2×18	4×12	2×16
	L	1×9	1×6	0×3
Medium (2)	H	1×18	1×12	1×6
	M	5×12	2×8	1×4
	L	2×6	0×4	0×2
Low (I)	H	0×9	0×6	1×3
	M	2×6	1×4	2×2
	L	1×3	0×2	0×1

H = High

M = Medium

L = Low

Appendix-II

Interview Schedule

Impact of Developmental Programmes on Empowerment of Mother and Girl Child

Beneficiary of scheme

Village Block District

General Information of the respondent

Name of the respondent: W/o or D/o

Profit of the respondent:

1. Age of respondent (years)

Young (20-30 years)	1
Middle (30-40 years)	2

2. Caste

General	1
BC	2
SC	3

3. Body mass index

Height

Weight

4. Educational qualification

Illiterate	0
Primary	1
Middle	2
High school	3

5. Type of family

Nuclear	1
Joint	2

6. Size of family

Small (upto 4 members)	1
Medium	2
Large (8 & more)	3

7. Order of children — Age — Sex

Order of children	Age	Sex
1.		
2.		
3.		

8. Occupation

Respondent

Husband

9. Family income (Below Poverty Line)

(a) Extremely poor (upto 10,000) 1

Very poor (10,000-20,000) 2

Poor (20,000-25,000) 3

(b) Land holding

Nil 0

Member of an organization 1

Office bearer 2

Public leader 3

Communication variable

11. Mass media exposure

No exposure	0
Radio	1
Television	2

12. Sources of information and motivation	Sources of information	Sources motivation
Cosmopolite		
Programme Officer		
C.D.P.O.		
Anganwadi Supervisor		
Anganwadi worker		
Bank officials		
Localite		
Relatives		
Friends		
Neighbours		
Sarpanch		

Knowledge regarding Different Aspects of 'Apni Beti Apna Dhan' Programme

		Nil Knowledge	Partial Knowledge	Complete Knowledge
1.	The benefit is given to girl child born on and after 2nd Oct, 1994.			
2.	The benefit is given upto 3 children in family.			
3.	The benefit is given to mothers of girl child only of BPL family.			

4. A benefit of Rs. 500/- is given to mother at the birth of girl child within 15 days for nutrition.

5. The benefit is for both rural and urban mothers and girl child.

6. The IVP of Rs. 2500/- is deposited in name of girl child within three months of the birth of girl child.

7. The IVP will mature after 18 years.

8. The IVP is given to girl child for higher education, starting some work or for marriage.

9. The form is given in rural areas by AWW and in urban areas in Civil Hospital, PHC, CHC.

10. The benefit in rural areas is given by I.C.D.S. supervisor and in urban areas by female workers of health department within 15 days of birth of girl child.

Knowledge Regarding Different Aspects of 'Balika Samridhi Yojana'

		Nil Knowledge	Partial Knowledge	Complete Knowledge
1.	The benefit is given to mother and girl child born on or after 15th August, 1997.			
2.	The benefit is availed by family BPL.			
3.	The benefit is upto 2 girl child in family BPL irrespective of the numbers of children in family.			
4.	A grant of Rs. 500/- is given to mother of a girl child in family BPL for better nutrition.			
5.	A post delivery grant of Rs. 500/- per girl child is deposited in the name of girl child in a post office/ bank.			
6.	The form is given by AWW/supervisor at village level.			
7.	The benefit is for both rural and urban mothers and girl child.			
8.	An annual scholarship from			

Rs.300/- for class I to Rs. 1000/- for class X when she goes to school is deposited in the account of girl child.

9. The deposit will mature when she attains the age of 18 years.

10. The girl child should be unmarried at the age of 18 years.

Knowledge Regarding Different Aspects of 'National Maternity Benefit Scheme'

		Nil Knowledge	Partial Knowledge	Complete Knowledge
1.	The benefit is availed by mother BPL.			
2.	The benefit is for both rural and urban mothers.			
3.	The benefit is availed upto 2 live births of children (boy/girl).			
4.	The age of pregnant women must be above 19 years.			
5.	An amount of Rs. 500/- is given to mother between 7 to 9 months of pregnancy for nutritious food.			
6.	The benefit is availed 8-12 weeks before the birth of child.			

7. The form is given by AWW in rural areas and by medical officer in urban areas.

8. The certificate of pregnancy is issues by A.N.M. in village.

9. The information in the form is certified by village Panchayat.

Attitude Towards the Developmental Programmes for Empowerment of Mother and Girl Child

		Strongly favourable	Favourable	Neutral	Unfavorable	Strongly unfavourable
1.	Developmental programmes are important for national development.					
2.	The developmntal programmes for mother and girl child are the need of the hour.					
3.	The developmental programmes with focus on girl child will help in balancing the adverse sex ratio.					
4.	The developmental programmes will motivate people in imparting edu-					

cation and increase in women's participation in economic activities.

5. The developmental programme for mother and girl child will help to delay the age of girls at marriage.

6. The developmental programme will help to bring down the birth rate.

7. The developmental programmes help in changed behaviour towards mother and girl child.

8. One should not avail the benefit of developmental programmes unless others in the village go for the same.

9. It is national wastage to spend money on developmental programmes.

10. The household survey (BPL) undertaken for the purpose of identification of beneficiary is satisfying.

11. The criteria for household survey (BPL) for identification is satisfying.

12. Availing the benefit of developmental programmes is very satisfying for mother and girl child.

13. To avail the benefit of these developmental programmes is a tedious job.

14. To avail the benefit of these developmental programmes is a tiring job.

15. The girl child is no more considered a burden on parents.

16. These programmes help in changing thinking of mothers and family towards girl child.

Utilization of Benefits of Developmental Programmes for Empowerment of Mother and Girl Child

1. How many times programme benefit was availed

   a) Once b) Twice c) More than two times

2. How much amount you were able to get?

   a) 100% b) 75-100% c) 50-75% d) Less than 50%

3. Did you have to spend extra expenditure in obtaining the benefit?

   Yes/No

4. How much time was taken by department for release of amount?

   a) Within stipulated period b) More than specified period of time

   Yes/No

5. BPL survey conducted
6. Satisfied with BPL survey
7. Amount adequate to meet nutritional requirements
8. Satisfied with the arrangement of amount distribution
9. Visit to anganwadi centres
10. Satisfied with services provided at Anganwadi Centres.
11. Motivated regarding family planning methods by village level ICDS functionaries
12. Visiting of village level ICDS functionaries
13. No. of visits of village level ICDS functionaries to house

    a) Once b) 2 times c) 3 times d) 4 times

Impact on Empowerment of Mother and Girl Child

Yes/No

a) Reduced mortality rate of girls

b) Change in attitude of family towards mother and girl child

c) To delay the age at marriage of girls atleast upto 18 years

d) To bring down birth rate

e) In imparting education to girl child

f) In improving nutritional status of mother and girl child

Constraints Faced in Utilization of Developmental Programmes for Empowerment of Mother and Girl Child

Yes/No

Organizational barriers

- Favouritism in selection of beneficiaries

- Insufficient staff in village i.e. AWW/ANM/Supervisor
- No coordination and linkage between village staff and staff at distt. headquarter
- Lack of guidance by grams panchayat regarding developmental programmes
- Favouritism in selection of BPL families

Economic barriers

- Lack of funds (Government)
- Delay in release of money
- Extra expenditure has to be paid for availing benefit
- Amount received not sufficient to meet requirements

Educational and communication barriers

- Lack of knowledge about schemes in operation
- Lack of knowledge about objectives of programmes
- Lack of literature and timely guidance
- Lack of encouragement and motivation
- No proper extension staff to communicate

Socio-cultural barriers

- Family responsibility and excessive burden of work
- Lack of motivation from family and society
- Husband takes away the money
- Hindrance due to ill health
- Poor chance of mobility for mother

Any other

Select Bibliography

Agarwal, D. (2001). "Empowerment of rural women in India". *Social Welfare*, 48(4): 3-4.

Ahlawat, Tripta (1999). *Impact of Financial Assistance Schemes on the Economic Empowerment of Women.* M.Sc. Thesis, H.A.U., Hisar.

Amin, S.K. (2001). `Why do girls dropout?' *Social Welfare*, 48(I):5-7.

Aneja, A. and Chhikara, S. (1994) Socio-personal factors of anganwadi workers as related to delivery of health and nutrition education. *Haryana Agric. Univ. J. Res.*, 24(2&3): 132-136.

Anonymous. (1980). *ICDS Scheme.* Ministry of Social Welfare, Government of India, New Delhi.

Anonymous (1987). Girl Child. *NIPCCD Newsletter*, 8(2): 12.

Anonymous, (1990). "Give the girl child her due." *Yojana*, 34(23): 8-14.

Azim, S. (2001). Gender empowerment—Where does India stand? *Social Welfare*, 48(2): 8-10.

Balishter and Umesh Chandra (1990). "Integrated Rural Development Programme: A Study in Etawa District in Uttar Pradesh." *Yojana*, 26-27.

Bhagania, V. (1996). "An exploratory study of the impact of economic development programme on rural women." M.Sc. Thesis, Hisar.

Bhatnagar, S. and Shakhin, D. (1979). "Anganwadi workers of ICDS projects as an agent of primary health care delivery." *Indian J. Pub. Hlth.*, 23(4): 214.

Bhatnagar, S. and Singhal, A. (1984). "Attitude of women participants towards ICDS programme." *Ind. J. Extn. Edn.*, Sept-Dec. XX(3&4): 67-68.

Bhogle, S. (1991). "Child rearing practices and behaviour development of a girl child." *Indian Journal Social Work*, 52(1): 61-69.

Boora, Pinky (1997). *Communication and Utilization Pattern of Nutritional and Educational Opportunities.* M.Sc. Thesis. H.A.U., Hisar.

Chakraboati, A.K., Gupta, J.P. and Tyagi, B.N. (1984). "Socio-psychological correlates in the adoption of health innovations among tribals within intensive service zone of PHC." Health and Population—Perspectives and Issues, 7(1):72-83.

Chamola, S.D., Sardana, P.K. and Patel, R.K. (1986). "Impact of 'TRYSEM' programmes on income and employment of women in district Hisar." Paper presented in the Seminar on 'Role of Development Programmes on Socio- economic Status of Women', held at Dept. of Agricultural Economics, March 21-22, H.A.U., Hisar.

Chander Mohan. (2001). Services for adolescent girls—An assessment. *Social Welfare*, 48(3): 3-7.

Chandra, S. Kohli (1996). *Women's Development: Problems and Prospects.* APH Publication Cooperation, New Delhi, pp 19-35.

Chatterji, S.A. (1988). *The Indian Women's Search for Identity.* Vikas Publishers, New Delhi, p. 146.

Chaudhary, D. Paul.(1990). What do we need to reduce their drudgery, *Kurukshetra*, 38(12).

Chaudhary, M.A. (1993). "Encouraging rural women to save." *Social Welfare,* 32(6):21-25.

Chhikara, S. (1982). Infant and maternal mortality and morbidity in one Integrated Child Development. I.C. College of Home Science, H.A.U., Hisar.

Chidambaran, K. and Themonzhi, G. (1998). "Constraints for women entrepreneurs", *Social Welfare,* 45(1): 28-31.

Dev. R. and Lal, B. (1989). Monitoring and evaluation of community participation in an ICDS project. *Research Abstracts of ICDS.* NIPCCD Publication, pp. 320-321.

Dhar, P. (1989). "ICDS—A participatory approach." *Yojana,* 1-15 Sept. 28-29.

Freire, P. (1979). In Sharma, A. (ed.). "Monitoring Social Components of Integrated Child Development Services," NIPCCD, p. 92.

Gangrade, K.D. (1966). "A sociological study of a village women centre," *Social Welfare,* 13(1):4.

Ghosh, S. (1991). "Girl child: A lifetime of deprivation and discrimination," *Indian Journal of Social Work,* 52(1):21-27.

Goyal, Seema. (1990). An analysis of rural health delivery services for rural women in Haryana: Communication and utilization pattern.

Gulati, U. (1995). Women's empowerment in India with special reference to rural women. Social Welfare, Aug. 17-19.

Gupta, Jugal and Machan da (1979). Functioning of anganwadi workers in Integrated Child Development Services Scheme, Jama Masjid, Delhi. *Health and Population—Perspectives and Issues.* 2(1):97-98.

Habibullah, M.I. (1987). Child marriage—Superstitions and widowhood extort a heavy price. *Social Welfare,* 34(1):13-27.

Jain, R. (1990). The stigma of being born as a girl. *Social Welfare,* 36(10-11): 21-23.

Jamal, S. (1984). Suitability of nutrition and home management practices and communication behaviour among farm women. M.Sc. Thesis (unpublished), G.B. Pant Univ. of Agri. and Tech., Pantnagar, Nainital.

Jayaweera, S. (1979). "Programmes of non-formal education for women." *Ind. J. Adult Edu.,* 40(12):33.

Jorapur, P.B. (1981). Integrated Health and Nutrition Programme. *Yojana,* 25(7):26-27.

Joshi, S.C. (1996). "Indira Mahila Yojana: Empowerment of Women." *Kurukshetra,* March. 24-30.

Kamath, M.S. (1991). "Malnutrition, the silent killer", *The Tribune,* Jan. 8, p. 4, Chandigarh.

Kant, S.K. (2001). "Women's empowerment and mutual cooperation in the family." *Social Welfare,* 48(1): 3-4.

Kaptan, S.S. (1994). "Towards a new dawn." *Social Welfare,* 40(11):3-7.

Kaur, G. and Narwal, R.S. (1988). "An immunization: A least adopted practice." *Ind. J. Pub. Health.,* 35(4):199-200.

Kulshrestha, I. (1990). "The story of every girl." *The Hindustan Times,* July, 14:7.

Kumar, A., Kumar, S. Mishra, C.P. and Tiwari, I.C. (1988). "Impact of community participation on level of maternal and child health care in rural area of Varanasi." *Ind. J. Pub. Health.,* 32(2):92-93.

Kumar, B.S., Ramaiah, P.V. (1992). "A study of the implementators and salient features of JRY." *Maha. J. Extn. Edn.,* 11(1):112.

Kumar, P. (1990). "Give children their due." *The Hindustan Times,* Nov. 10:8.

Mathur, S. (1984). "Boy or girl." *Social Welfare*, 31(1):28-29.

Mehindale, S.M., Karandikar, V.N. and Natu, M.N. (1982). Role of ICDS in the delivery of certain MCH services—ICDS areas. Research on ICDS: An overview. 1 1975-85. NIPCCD. pp 325-326.

Mehta, S.R. (1971). Community development programme: Some reaction of village leaders. *Community Dev. and Panchayati Raj Digest*. 3(4):340-342.

Nagarjan, N. (1998). Eco-technological Intervention for farm women. *Social Welfare*, 45(1): 14-17.

Nair, R. (1989). An evaluation study done to find out the impact of ICDS on tribal women with reference to health and nutrition of Shahpur Taluka, Research Abstracts on ICDS, NIPCCD Publications, 1989. Managerial Stop gaps in the delivery of ante-natal care services in rural areas of Varanasi. *Ind. J. Pub. Health.*, 33(3):126-127.

Narayanan, L. (1989). Indepth study on community participation in ICDS. Paper from National Conference on Research on ICDS. NIPCCD Publications, pp. 311-312.

Natarajan, T. (1989). Bird's eye view of 'Antenatals'. ICDS Project 3 Madras, Tamil Nadu. *Research Abstracts on ICDS*, NIPCCD Publications, pp. 238-239.

NIPCCD. (2000). *Report—Girl of Today* —Woman of tomorrow.

NPA. (1992). *National Plan of Action for Chiidren*, NIPCCD Report (2000).

Padmanabhan, A.S., Ganga, N., Elango, V. and Swaminathan, P. (1989). *Parental Attitude Towards Immunization*. Research Abstracts on ICDS, NIPCCD Publications, pp. 124-125.

Paranjpe, R.K. and Bhagwat, R. (1986). "A Study of perception and participation of the community in ICDS—Maharashtra State, Unpublished Mimeographed, College of Social Work, Nirmala Niketan Bombay. In *Research Abstracts on ICDS*, NIPCCD Publications, pp. 314-315.

Planning Department, Government of Haryana. 2000. *Evaluation Study of "Apni Beti Apna Dhan" in Haryana.*

Ponnuraj, S. (1994). "Community participation for health of mothers and children." *World Health Forum,* 15(3):272.

Prasad, C.M. (1995). Development of Women and Children in rural areas: Successful case studies. *J. Rural Dev.* 14(1): 65-87.

Rajula Devi, A.K. (1986). "Poverty in rural areas—A study." *Kurukshetra,* 34(5):13.

Ramchandran, L. (1977). A study on district health administration. *Health and Population—Perspectives and Issues,* 1(1):88-89.

Rao, K.P.C. (1987). "Rural Development: A Case Study in A.P." *Kurukshetra* 35(5):4.

Rao, V.M. (1997). "Giving Control into Women's Hand." *Social Welfare,* 45(2):7-8.

Rohtagi, S. (1983). "Marriage before the age of consent." *Social Welfare,* 29(10)3.

Salvi, G. (1989). "The Lesser Child", *The Hindustan Times,* Nov. 23:2.

Sethi, D.P. (1976). *The SNP in Delhi: A case study of benefit delivery and utilization.* NIPCCD, New Delhi.

Sharma, N.K. and Sharma, K.D. (1998). "Utilization of Information sources at different stages of adoption." *Maha J. Extn. Edn.* XVII:207-214.

Sharma, O.P. (1987). "Child marriage on the decline in Jammu and Kashmir," *Social Welfare,* 34(1): 14-15.

Sharma, P. (2001). "A flicker of hope." *Social Welfare,* 48(1): 40.

Shekhar, M.C. (1975). *Special Child Relief Programme—An Observational Study.* Council for Social Development, New Delhi.

Singhal, S. and Goyal, M. (1986). "A study on decision making practices regarding family financial resource on household expenditure." *Journal of Research H.A.U.*, 16(2): 183-185.

Singh, O.R. (2001). "Education and women's empowerment," *Social Welfare*, 48(1): 35-36.

Sood, A. (1994). "Development of rural women—Perception and outcome." *Kurukshetra*, 42(12):15-18.

Sud, S. (1982). "Let's leave it to people's better judgement," *Kurukshetra*, 31(1): 54-55.

Sundaram, S.I. (2001), "Education and empowerment of village women", *Social Welfare*, 48(2):3-5.

Sundri, S., Kamalambai (1991). "Women in TRYSEM: A case study". *Yojana*, 35(3): 21-25.

Tripathi, P. (1989). "Women workers in urban unorganised sector." *Social Welfare*, 36(2):23.

Trivedi, G. (1982). "The why and how of people participation." *Kurukshetra*, 31(1):63-65.

UN Convention. (1992). "UN Convention on the Rights of the Child Welfare", *India 2000*, p. 279.

Venkataramana, M. (1995). "A case study on DWCRA in Andhra," *Social Welfare*, 42(3): 12-15.

Verma, U. (1987) *An Analysis of Communication Disseminating and Information Utilizing Systems of Home Science in Haryana.* Ph.D. Thesis, Haryana Agri. Univ., Hisar.

Vidulata (1989). *Impact of TRYSEM Programme on Status of Women,* Ph.D. Thesis, H.A.U., Hisar.

Index

N

P

Q

R

S

□□□